"In this compelling new book, practical insights and suggestions for supporting the education of Latino students are offered and supported with evidence. For educators who are searching for strategies to improve the academic performance of Latino students, this book could not be more timely. We are living at a time when immigrant students generally, and Latino students specifically, are increasingly under attack and scrutiny. For this reason, this book will be an invaluable resource who seek to use education to make a difference."

—**Pedro A. Noguera**, *Distinguished Professor of Education, UCLA*

"This book offers hope for school leaders who are truly dedicated to the education of ALL students. It offers specific strategies and examples from schools around the United States who are truly meeting the needs of Latino students and making good on the promise of equality."

—**Anthony Muhammad**, *Author and Educational Consultant, New Frontier 21*

Five Practices for Improving the Success of Latino Students

Based on the work of real leaders and educators in high-performing, urban schools across the country, this book unpacks five key practices that are integral to improving achievement and postsecondary outcomes for Latino students. These inspiring stories affirm that excellence and equity are possible when educators come together around an important purpose and focus on the needs, strengths, and interests of all their students. Full of specific examples and guidance, each chapter also includes an assessment tool designed to help school leaders reflect upon their current practices, affirm school strengths that resemble the exemplary practices described in the chapters, and help educators pinpoint opportunities to strengthen practices in ways that can improve the postsecondary readiness of their students. This important book will help leaders create a positive school culture, coherent school design, and develop the practices and policies that support Latino students in their performance and help students realize their potential.

Christina Theokas, Ph.D., is Director of Research at the National Center for Urban School Transformation at San Diego State University, USA.

Mary L. González, Ed.D., has 28 years of experience in public education. She recently retired from the San Diego County Office of Education as a Program Specialist, overseeing the Migrant Education Program in various school districts in North San Diego County, USA.

Consuelo Manriquez, Ed.D., is Associate Director of Communications and Operations at Darnall Charter School in San Diego, USA.

Joseph F. Johnson, Jr., Ph.D., is Dean of the College of Education, Executive Director of the National Center for Urban School Transformation, and the QUALCOMM Professor of Urban Education at San Diego State University, USA.

Other Eye On Education Books
Available from Routledge
(www.routledge.com/eyeoneducation)

Five Practices for Improving the Success of Latino Students

A Guide for Secondary School Leaders

Christina Theokas,
Mary L. González,
Consuelo Manriquez, and
Joseph F. Johnson, Jr

Routledge
Taylor & Francis Group

NEW YORK AND LONDON

First published 2019
by Routledge
711 Third Avenue, New York, NY 10017

and by Routledge
2 Park Square, Milton Park, Abingdon, Oxon, OX14 4RN

Routledge is an imprint of the Taylor & Francis Group, an informa business

Library of Congress Cataloging-in-Publication Data
A catalog record for this title has been requested

ISBN: 978-1-138-71360-4 (hbk)
ISBN: 978-1-138-71361-1 (pbk)
ISBN: 978-1-315-19858-3 (ebk)

Typeset in Optima
by Florence Production Ltd, Stoodleigh, Devon, UK

Contents

Contents

Acknowledgments

This book is a celebration of the outstanding teachers, administrators, and support staff at Eastlake High School in the Socorro Independent School District in El Paso, Texas; The O'Farrell High School in San Diego, California; James Pace Early College High School in the Brownsville Independent School District in Brownsville, Texas; and Revere High School in the Revere Public School District in Boston, Massachusetts. We admire, respect, and acknowledge your accomplishments. You inspire us to keep identifying, studying and telling the stories of amazing schools like yours. Also, we appreciate your willingness to open your schools to us and allow us to learn from your work. We hope this book does justice to your impressive accomplishments and motivates you to continue striving for excellence.

We also acknowledge and appreciate the many individuals; including school administrators, graduate students, professors and teachers who have engaged with us in visiting and studying America's high-performing urban schools. Your time, energy and insights have been priceless, as we have sought to better understand teaching and learning in outstanding urban schools.

We must also acknowledge that the study of high-performing urban schools is not new. Our work builds upon a tradition of scholarship and inquiry started by heroic educators like Ron Edmonds, Larry Lezotte, and Wilbur Brookover and extended through the work of others such as Pedro Noguera, Patricia Gandara, James Scheurich, Karin Chenoweth, Mike Schmoker, Kati Haycock, Linda Skrla, Kathryn McKenzie, and others. These leaders constructed the foundation upon which this effort was built.

We especially acknowledge the strong support of San Diego State University. The former university president, Stephen Weber, and the former dean of the university's college of education, Lionel "Skip" Meno envisioned a national center that would identify, study and promote excellence in urban schools. They secured initial funding support from the QUALCOMM Corporation, and they creatively sought/provided other support that helped us start the National Center for Urban School Transformation (NCUST). As an expression of their commitment to urban K-12 education, the university has continued this strong support, even in difficult financial times. The advocacy and support of the current university president, Sally Roush, and the current provost, Chukuka S. Enwemeka, have helped NCUST thrive and grow.

Finally, we acknowledge the time, wisdom and commitment of our colleagues and staff at San Diego State University and at NCUST. We are honored to work with and learn from individuals who have committed themselves to supporting America's urban schools.

Meet the Authors

Christina Theokas, Ph.D. is Director of Research at the National Center for Urban School Transformation. Christina has more than 25 years of experience working or conducting research in schools including as a special education teacher, psychologist, supervisor of curriculum, assessment and training, principal and director of research and evaluation. In addition, she was the Chief Program Officer for an out of school time provider and Director of Research at The Education Trust where she co-authored a book on school leadership in high-performing, high-poverty schools, *Getting it Done: Leading Academic Success in Unexpected Schools*. Her other research and publications focus on positive youth development, high school reform, teacher equity, rigorous assignments and understanding gaps at the high end of achievement.

Mary Gonzales, Ed.D. conducted the exploratory study, for her doctoral dissertation at San Diego State University, that led to the research for this book. Mary has 28 years of experience in public education. She has served as a middle school and high school teacher and she has held various leadership roles, such as Assistant Director for the Student Academic Services Outreach Program office at California State University San Marcos, working primarily to help under-represented middle and high school students enter higher education institutions. She recently retired from the San Diego County Office of Education as a Program Specialist, overseeing the Migrant Education Program in various school districts in North San Diego County.

Consuelo Manriquez, Ed.D. is Associate Director of Communications and Operations at Darnall Charter School. She began her career as a teacher in Los Angeles in 1989. Since then, Consuelo has served as a bilingual teacher, Title I resource teacher, technology coordinator, vice-principal and principal in various schools in San Diego. In her work, she demonstrated success in accelerating the achievement of all students and in particular, English Language Learners. Her doctoral dissertation at San Diego State University, *Turnaround Schools: A Comparative Studies of Two Small High Schools*, examined key issues that increased student achievement in the Latino Student population.

Joseph F. Johnson, Jr., Ph.D., is Dean of the College of Education, Executive Director of the National Center for Urban School Transformation and the QUALCOMM Professor of Urban Education within the department of educational leadership at San Diego State University. He previously served as a teacher, school and district administrator, state education agency administrator, researcher and technical assistance provider and as a Senior Executive Service Director at the US Department of Education. He has published multiple articles, books, book chapters and reports on schools and districts that achieve remarkable academic results for diverse populations of students including, *Teaching Practices from America's Best Urban Schools* and *Leadership in America's Best Urban Schools*.

Preface

High school represents a critical time in young lives. During these years, students begin to explore what they want to do and be as adults and the foundation for fulfilling lives and meaningful civic participation is laid. Despite the diligent work of school leaders, educators, and advocates, on average, academic performance in high schools has remained stagnant for decades and achievement and attainment gaps persist between student groups (NCES, 2015). Camille Farrington, in her book, *Failing at School: Lessons for Redesigning Urban High Schools*, argues, ". . . so many students fail out of school not because of their own flawed characters or intellectual inadequacies, but because high schools were designed in a way that produces widespread failure" (pg. 3). In particular, both graduation rates and dropout rates suggest that urban high schools are not designed to support Latino students who are the least likely to graduate and most likely to drop out of school.

Although the recent trend in graduation rate data is positive and there are fewer "dropout factories," urban high schools still struggle to provide students, and particularly Latino students, with the strong foothold they need to move successfully to postsecondary education and employment (America's Promise Alliance, 2015; Bromberg & Theokas, 2016). We understand high schools that serve students in low-income, urban communities face real challenges, but these public institutions are critically important if we want to change the patterns in the data and the trajectory of young peoples' lives. Excellent high schools can provide sturdy safety nets that reduce the likelihood that Latino students drop out of school, achieve at low levels, and perpetuate cycles of poverty. And, they can also be the force that propels students towards futures they might not have even imagined. As one high student told us,

> One of the teachers that really, really helped me change
> who I used to be and become the way I am right now is Mr.
> Basil. He's always seeing something in me that I guess I
> never saw in myself. I really appreciate that because I was
> really rude to him. I had the worst attitude when I was a
> freshman and a sophomore. Now, I'm going to college . . .
> If I had changed schools when I wanted to, I wouldn't be
> who I am right now.

Or, as another student told us,

> I feel like this high school has prepared me for college and
> for the outside world. I feel like if I didn't come here, I mean,
> I'd be completely lost for college. I probably wouldn't have
> gone to college or anything.

In this book, we profile four excellent high schools that have helped Latino youth (as well as youth from other demographic groups) achieve impressive academic results, as well as strong engagement in co-curricular and extra-curricular areas that have broadened their knowledge and interests and provided experiences for their future success. Educators in these schools have put structures and supports in place to ensure all students, regardless of race/ethnicity, class, economics, and language background are well prepared upon graduation for a wide variety of postsecondary options. They are not just graduating more students or selecting some students for rigorous learning opportunities; they are providing all students access to a challenging curriculum and caring relationships that help students realize their potential. In particular, we selected these four high schools based on their belief in and success with Latino students who are defying long-standing patterns of low achievement and student disengagement as documented by Gandara and Contreras (2010) and coined the Latino Education Crisis.

The national data are sobering. Too many Latino children in the American school system enter behind and most never catch up. Beginning in pre-school and continuing through high school, Latino students underachieve academically, leading to increasing gaps in postsecondary education and the lowest earnings among all racial/ethnic groups (Carnevale & Fasules, 2017; Education Trust West, 2017; Gandara &

Contreas, 2010; Gandara, 2010). This is despite the fact that Latino families have a strong work ethic, an intense desire to succeed, an understanding of the value and utility of education, and a trust and belief in the quality of the American school system (Hill & Torres, 2010; Lopez, 2001; Suarez-Orozco & Suarez-Orozco, 1995). Unfortunately, Latino parents often lack the knowledge and experience in U.S. schools and colleges to guide their children toward postsecondary education and productive careers. For example, U.S. census data shows that more than 40 percent of Latina mothers do not have a high school diploma; and only about 10 percent of Latina mothers have a college degree or higher (Gandara, 2010). Schools are therefore essential; they can offer what parents and communities cannot and fill the gap so that Latino students can achieve their goals. To that point, research has shown that school benefits poor children more than middle-class children (Alexander, Entwisle, & Olsen, 1997; Coleman, 1966). Further, Gandara (2010) asserts, "Under the right conditions, schools could conceivably close the gaps for Latino children, but the schools that serve most Latino students today have not met those conditions." (p.26). These four urban high schools have. The educators in the four featured schools have confronted these challenges with the belief that ensuring the success of Latino students is of utmost importance. These educators are determined to break down barriers and build the bridge to their students' and families' dreams and aspirations.

This book presents what we learned from leaders, faculty, staff, students, and parents in these high schools and means to provide practical, useful information that can help other educators ensure the success of their Latino students. We set out to understand the leadership and culture that provided the foundation of excellence and equity in each of these schools and the practices, systems and policies they employed to help each and every student reach their goals. We also endeavored to identify and describe in detail the common characteristics found across all four schools. The chapters are organized around the core systems in high schools and across these structures, we identify five key practices as essential to each school's success. Our data do not support assumptions of causal impact, but we hope they highlight to other educators the more important factors to consider when redesigning their own schools. In sum, we see the story of these four urban high schools as compelling evidence that these learning outcomes are possible in far more schools and we believe they light the path forward for educators striving to do this work in their own schools.

Intended Audience

This book is about high schools that have achieved excellent learning results for Latino students. We expect that this book will be useful to principals, other school level administrators, superintendents, other district level administrators, and teacher leaders (including lead teachers, department chairs, resource teachers, helping teachers, team leaders, and educators who provide support for teachers) in schools and districts that serve Latino high school students. This volume is intended to be useful to leaders (or future leaders) who strive to influence the academic success of Latino students. While our focus was on secondary schools and schools that achieved exemplary outcomes for Latino students, we believe the lessons learned are applicable to all schools and schools serving other demographic populations. The five practices that emerged as essential capitalize on key systems and structures present in all schools and also the characteristics and behaviors of leaders that are well documented in other research, both in education and in other fields. We believe the stories and examples are rich and compelling and will help other educators reflect on their schools and identify strengths and areas to be improved.

Contents of the Book

To set the context for our findings, Chapter One begins with a description of the Latino education crisis, outlining documentation of the persistent opportunity, achievement, and attainment gaps Latino youth experience. As contrast, we share some of the findings about the characteristics of highly effective urban schools and specifically practices that have proven to be successful with Latino students combatting the harsh statistics documented by researchers. This rich research and data provided the backdrop as we developed our methodology to learn specifically about high schools that helped prepare Latino students for exciting and full futures. We share our methods to identify the schools we studied and also the tools and approach to collect and triangulate data from various stakeholders that led to the identification of the five practices that were common across schools. Chapter One concludes with detailed profiles of each of the four high schools we studied (three comprehensive public high schools and one public charter high school).

Chapter Two is devoted to descriptions of leadership in the four schools. Leithwood, Louis, Anderson, and Wahlstrom (2004) reported, "Indeed, there are virtually no documented instances of troubled schools being turned around in the absence of intervention by talented leaders. Many other factors may contribute to such turnarounds, but leadership is the catalyst" (p. 5). Similarly, we found that leadership was a major catalyst to the success of Latino students in the four schools. In Chapter Two, we describe the leaders' vision and actions and in particular how they rely on other administrators, teachers, and staff to come together as a team and influence the improvement of teaching and learning to ensure student preparation for postsecondary. In the four schools, leadership responsibilities do not rest within a single individual; the school leaders rally their team around an important goal and vision for their school and distribute leadership broadly. This was the first practice- an important goal, and second practice- shared ownership. These two practices bookended the work done at the schools. An important purpose guided the work and each stakeholder felt responsible for accomplishing the tasks associated with their role that supported accomplishment of their goals. Each school has a brand that is known, loved and fought for by all. Decades of research have documented the importance of school climate and culture and these schools are no different. Chapter Two illustrates the role leaders play in influencing the climate and culture of the school and unleashing the potential of all educators and students.

In Chapter Three, we discuss the student-centered values that guide decision-making in these schools. These values and their integration in school routines, practices, and policies were the second practice that laid the foundation of success for each of the four schools. The regular reinforcement of student-centered values and efforts to build relationships among students and staff helped each school establish an environment in which Latino students felt that they were valued by teachers, administrators, and other school personnel. Of particular importance, educators in each of the four schools made many efforts to demonstrate an appreciation of the cultural and linguistic diversity of their students and their families. Students felt like they belonged and were willing to work hard to learn important concepts and skills despite the many barriers placed in front of them. Further, belonging extended to all stakeholders as they felt like important and valued partners in the education of their students.

Chapters Four, Five, and Six describe how leaders utilized different elements of the instructional system (e.g., the master schedule, teacher collaboration, professional development, assessment of mastery, intervention, and enrichment) to support excellent teaching and learning and ensure student needs were met. Not only were students needs met, each of the schools was committed to providing rich and extensive opportunities to students to broaden their world view and help them build meaningful skills; this was the fourth key practice identified in the data. Although elements of the instructional system are described individually across the chapters, the most important lesson we learned was that the systems were coherent and aligned with the school goals and vision established. Choices and decisions were always made, "in the best interest of students." This coherent school design was the final practice we identified as essential to each schools' success. It supported both students and teachers to focus on what was most important, continuously improve and achieve their goals.

In our final chapter, we bring together the elements discussed in each of the prior chapters and provide a map for educators that illustrates the five key practices en route to excellent results for Latino students. It is not a recipe or checklist, nor do we pretend that this work is easy, but there are key principles and practices that are worthy of attention and emulation. As well, we realize the structures and systems described in Chapter Two through Six are not distinct elements; they are part of a cohesive whole that influence and are influenced by one another. We hope to deepen understanding of how improvement and excellence happens by harnessing typical school processes, building coherence, maintaining focus, and intentionally seeking specific outcomes.

Each chapter includes a brief assessment tool. These tools were designed to help school leaders and educators assess and reflect upon their current practices, their impact on all students and Latino students in particular. The assessment tools will affirm school strengths that resemble the exemplary practices described in the chapters. As well, the assessment tools will help educators pinpoint opportunities to strengthen practices in ways that can improve the success of all students, and particularly Latino students. The assessments were designed to assist committed educators in focusing upon and assessing the subtle nuances that may make a major difference in the success of many Latino students. We hope the questions support constructive efforts to improve practices, programs and policies in ways that improve learning outcomes for Latino students.

Conclusion

In sum, critics would have us believe that excellence and equity do not coexist in urban education. They suggest that urban schools can successfully pursue excellence for an elite few or they can pursue educational mediocrity, focused on low-level standards for all. In contrast, in major cities across the country, we have found some high schools (albeit a relatively small number) where all groups of students achieve at high levels, are ready for postsecondary education and training, and are eager to take on new challenges. We believe that these schools and educators deserve our praise, celebration and study. This book endeavors to celebrate, inspire, and provide detailed descriptions of practices, in ways that illustrate that academic excellence and readiness for college and careers can be attained for all groups of students. As Blankstein and Noguera (2015) argued, we have found that "equity and excellence are not at odds, and that the highest level of excellence will actually be obtained *through* the pursuit of equity" (p. 5).

References

Alexander, K., Entwisle, D., & Olsen, L. (1997). *Children, schools, and inequality*. Boulder, CO: Westview Press.

America's Promise Alliance. (2015). *Building a grad nation: Progress and challenge in raising high school graduation rates*. Washington, DC: America's Promise Alliance.

Blankstein, A. M., & Noguera, P. (2015). *Excellence through equity: Five principles of courageous leadership to guide achievement for every student*. Thousand Oaks, CA: Corwin.

Bromberg, M., & Theokas, C. (2013). *Falling out of the lead: Tracking high achievers through high school and beyond*. Washington, DC: The Education Trust.

Carnevale, A., & Fasules, M. (2017). *Latino education and economic progress: Running faster but still behind*. Washington, DC: Georgetown University, Center on Education and the Workforce.

Coleman, J. (1966). *Equality of educational opportunity*. Washington, DC: U.S. Government Printing Office.

The Education Trust West. (2017). *The majority report: Supporting the educational success of Latino students in California*. Oakland, CA Education Trust West.

Farrington, C. (2014). *Failing at school: Lessons for redesigning urban high schools*. Cambridge, MA: Harvard Education Press.

Gándara P., & Contreras, F. (2010). *The Latino education crisis: The consequences of failed social policies*. Cambridge, MA: Harvard University Press.

Gándara P. (2010). Special topic: The Latino education crisis. *Educational Leadership, 67*(5), 24–30.

Hill, N. E., & Torres, K. (2010). Negotiating the American dream: The paradox of aspirations and achievement about Latino students and engagement between their families and schools. *Journal of Social Issues, 66*(1), 95–112.

Leithwood, K., Louis, K. S., Anderson, S., & Wahlstrom, K. (2004). *Review of research: How leadership influence student learning*. New York: The Wallace Foundation.

Lopez, G. R. (2001). The value of hard work: Lessons on parent involvement from an

(im)migrant household. *Harvard Educational Review, 71*, 416–37.

National Center for Education Statistics (NCES). (2015). *The Condition of Education, 2015*. Washington, DC: U.S. Government Printing Office.

Suarez-Orozco, C., & Suarez-Orozco, M. (1995). *Transformations: Migration, family life, and achievement motivation among Latino adolescents*. Stanford, CA: Stanford University Press.

Voices from the Schools

Perhaps, the best way to share what this book is about is to share the voices of students, parents, teachers and administrators at the four high schools we had the privilege to study. Their words can be found elsewhere throughout this book, with additional context; however, we think this brief sampling explains why we believe there is so much to be learned from these impressive schools. Their words help illuminate the reasons behind the successes of Latino students at these schools.

Voices of Latino Students

"Teachers go overboard to help you."

"A lot of the teachers are really enthusiastic about the subject they teach, which helps a lot with learning the class."

"They will adjust their schedule for you. So if you can't make it at a certain time, they'll come in early or they will come after school to help you."

"It's a place kids can go if they have complaints or comments about the school; it gives you a voice. They teach you how to take action and make changes, rather than just complain."

"Teachers are doing this [providing tutoring on Saturdays] for us. We can at least show up."

"Advisory is always that time where we can talk to our advisory teacher. She's kind of like our mom and she kind of reminds us of what we have to do. She's my confidence booster and I don't know—I just love advisory. Other than lunch, that's probably my favorite part of the day."

"They say, 'we're not here to force you guys to go to college. We're here to make sure you guys are ready for college, and in case you choose not to go, you have a back-up plan.' You're still prepared for it [college] though."

"The administrators support us. They walk into our room and they ask, 'How are you guys?' They always pump us up. We have the support from administration and our teachers. They are all so dedicated."

"We all support each other. Students support students, teachers support students, and our principals support everyone. Our assistant principals are always at games and are always in the classroom making sure we are learning. They want to see we are really working, and I think that's really good support, like knowing that they care about us."

"Probably, something I like most about the teachers here is that they're always there to help."

"They always give you great advice and always push you to go further, so you reach your potential basically."

"My favorite class is math in general. I really love numbers and all that. But my favorite teacher is Ms. Chan. She's my English teacher. She teaches us AP literature. It's an opportunity that they're giving to us this year and I feel proud of myself."

Voices of Latino Parents

"There have been times when I come to open house, I come to activities, and administration is always telling us 'tell us what you need.' We are given that comfort to come, at any time, to them."

"They make you feel welcome. They always have a smile on their face. They're always interested in what's going on in your life and telling you what's going on in the building."

"One thing that had a great impact on me was the first day of classes. Everyone was greeting us. Everyone gave me a nice welcome even if they didn't know me. Everyone was saying 'Good morning, how can we help you? Are you new, are you looking for a particular room?' That had a big impact on me, the way they treated you."

"I hadn't seen a principal waiting outside to greet students and here, at the high school level, Mr. Rainey is out there every day. They try to know students by their name as well as the parents, 'Good morning, Ms. Mendoza.' It is like a family, like a small family, comfortable and friendly."

Voices of Support Staff

"We really, really, really focus on the family and make sure students are ok at home, so they can focus here at school."

"And, we always treat the students with respect, that's the biggest one. Treat the student with respect. Treat them as family."

"Everybody is respectful. Everything comes, in my point of view, from administrators in how they treat the kids. And from the administration, it goes to the teachers, staff, everyone. And that's what kids see and that's why they're good."

"We see ourselves in them and that's why they open up to us. And, that is how we can help them more. We understand what they are going through . . . you know, at home, and we tell them what they can do."

". . . Being here is completely different than being in Mexico. Knowing that people understand is helpful . . . I was a second-language learner and so when students come to me I'm able to understand and empathize. And when I say, 'You want to learn English? Let's work on it,' students feel supported."

"If a student does not like one class, it can ruin their whole day and make them not want to be here. So, we change it. We don't penalize kids. We try to find what they are interested in."

"One goal I have is around data literacy. I want to help our teachers become researchers in their classrooms and think like researchers. I want to help them use data to inform their instruction in meaningful ways and personalize instruction in a way that accelerates all students' academic achievement."

Voices of Teachers

"Success is the standard on our campus; excelling is the standard. We set that standard and we don't let them [students] believe they can't achieve it."

"Administrators, teachers, and the students are all collaborating toward a shared goal of helping our kids to get in and through college or to and through some sort of post-high school plans where they are committed and are successful. We all share that vision, we're given a voice, and we are able to exercise creative liberties to achieve that goal."

"We process data almost immediately every period. 'What's his strength? What's yours?' And we tweak instruction every period. We are actually grouped into grade level sections, like the sophomores are in one area, freshman teachers in another. So, for my team, we're all within four doors of each other so we meet every period just informally, but we tweak throughout the day and make adjustments for the benefit of the students."

"We're using programs like Illuminate to compare data. So it's not just, 'Oh, this works for me because it was really fun.' Instead we look at student results and identify strengths. There's a lot of data . . . but it's balanced. Teachers are allowed to use their intuition, but it has to be backed up with data and student success."

"I really feel like my students are part of my team. We are all working towards the same goal. I think about my AP class for example. We are all

there, we are working and I am helping them and they are helping me. We are growing together and we're in it, really in it together."

"We have a lot of autonomy to work with the state standards, but teach them the way we feel best . . . There is a lot of flexibility to adapt curriculum to what's going on in the world, to address what's going on locally, nationally, globally and really bring that in."

"Focusing on three particular things, I think, has really calmed some people's nerves and allowed people to really dig deeper."

"We try to be intentional. Let's try this. Let's do this. It's like a lab to hone our craft."

"When I first started working here in 1996, they would bring in a lot of outside people to tell us stuff, [and call it 'professional development']. Now teachers run almost all of our directors' meetings. So, for example, I'm taking one on writing that's being taught by two of my colleagues, and it's probably the best director's meeting I have ever done in my life. It goes by quickly and I can't wait for it to happen."

"At the beginning of each year, I meet the parents in my program. This was the [initial meeting] date. Well, five of my students and parents couldn't make it. So then, I set up several additional meetings, as I tried to reach all the parents. Then, some still couldn't make it. Then, I called the individual parents to see what was convenient. I asked, 'When is it good for you to come in?'"

"I have students in my room whose first language or home language is Spanish, and so, in class . . . there's no like—how do I say this—the world doesn't stop if someone starts speaking Spanish."

". . . What keeps us going are the relationships. Not just between teachers and students but also between teachers and other teachers. . . . It's a true passion project. We want to do it, and we take initiative to start new committees or new projects that we think would benefit our students."

"It is really nice that we are supported in how we grow. We can see it and not just talk about it in our meetings. To visually see what is happening in other classrooms helps me understand how it works."

"I think what's great is that there is a lot of collegiality between the faculty. Within any department, we get along really well. There is a mixture of veteran teachers, relatively new teachers. There are a lot of great ideas being shared across the board, and you see many similarities across classrooms. There is co-teaching, co-planning, and students getting really great instruction in the classroom."

"I think our kids feel a part of something. They know that they're missed when they're not here. We just really care about our kids, like a lot. We notice when they're not here."

"Discipline is a teachable moment. Kids need to know that when there is misbehavior, there is a consequence. But when you do discipline, there's a conversation. It's having a conversation because it is about having kids talk it out." He further explained, "We're trying to help them become adults."

Voices of Administrators

"The key to our kids' success in education is our teachers. You must have the best instruction, all the time. All our teachers want is to be supported. That's all they want, so that's our job. We provide that support."

"I walk into classrooms all the time. Every day, I step into a classroom, even if it's just taking the temperature. I look around constantly. I have formal walk-through observations that I do and informal evaluation observations, but I am just out there constantly."

"We really embrace the language they bring, the culture they bring, even the academic background they bring, and we honor those things ... Diversity is our strength!"

"It [Homebase] is our first way of making sure every kid is known and loved. And then beyond that, every teacher works on their teacher–student relationships in their classrooms, so that there aren't any cracks for kids to fall through."

"Do it one time and how do you expect teachers to learn. You have to come back to it and each time get a deeper understanding so that it can become old-hat."

"We have to choose—we can't keep teaching the way we were. I know you are passionate about what you do, but we have to change to meet the needs of our kids now."

"What can we do to make it better? How can we help you?" Help us help you. That's what we've learned from her. That's a school of thought that we follow. It is all about helping and serving."

"We're like the Marines; we leave no man behind."

"We just take them under our wing, and they're part of our family now . . . We work side by side. It's not us and them. No. It's all of us."

"Leadership is based on collaboration and shared decision making."

"Lots of love and a lot of care goes into what we do. Students come first . . . Students know it and when they see that there's a caring heart, it makes a lot of difference."

"If our teachers are actively engaged in teaching, students will be actively engaged in learning, minimizing any classroom disruptions or behaviors. It [discipline] goes hand-in-hand with classroom instruction. As a campus, administrators provide professional development and feedback to teachers about instruction so that engagement is high in the classroom and then we do not have to deal with discipline at a high scale."

"Students must have the chance at the best and be expected to be the best. They're capable."

"If you think, 'Oh, these poor kids,' and therefore, 'I must lower the standards because they don't have the same opportunities.' That is a disservice to the student.,' How do you say to somebody, 'Because you've had a difficult time, I'm not going to teach you to a high standard.?'"

"It's our commitment, it's from the teachers, from the parents, from the students, from everybody. It's all about the commitment and the dedication that we put in this job."

"It used to be, 'Here's the data. Let's move on.' To now, 'Here's the data, what is it telling us? What's our action plan? What are we doing next to make sure that all the students in the classroom meet the benchmarks and get the support needed?'"

"Every day we get two, three, four, or five kids coming. Most of the kids are coming from Latin American countries. We have 30 languages spoken in the school."

"For me, [data is] everything, to the point where I think sometimes teachers run away from me when they see me coming at them with Excel sheets."

"The rigor couldn't come in unless we made it relevant."

"Every kid on this planet has the same value and the same worth. And every kid deserves the same education ... It doesn't matter where you grow up. It doesn't matter what your last name is. It doesn't matter what you look like or whether you have a dad at home or not. Every kid deserves the same education."

Illustrations

Introduction

The Education of Latino Youth in American High Schools

High schools are a ubiquitous part of American adolescent life and culture and are critically important public institutions. They provide the bridge to students' futures and have the capacity to change the trajectory of students' lives. Unfortunately, the data show stagnant outcomes for high schools over time and persistent gaps in achievement for students from different racial ethnic groups (See Figures 1.1 and 1.2). In particular, the gap in outcomes for Latino students motivated our study. We conduct a systematic analysis of successful urban schools serving predominantly Latino students to more deeply understand their school design and strategies that lead to their success. We hope to advance a common understanding of what is necessary for high schools to improve, in general, and in particular for Latino students so more schools can boast similar outcomes.

The Data

The opportunity gap and resulting achievement and attainment gaps between Latino students and their peers is well documented. Frequently cited examples of disparities are noted in various standardized measures of academic achievement, high school graduation and dropout rates and college matriculation and success. Although progress has been made in the last decade for Latino youth, large gaps still exist on almost any indicator examined. For example, on the National Assessment of Educational Progress, only 25 percent of twelfth grade Latino students are proficient in reading; 12 percent are proficient in mathematics (NCES, 2015). Latino students underperform their White peers by nearly 20 percentage points in both subjects. Similarly, although the high school graduation rate has

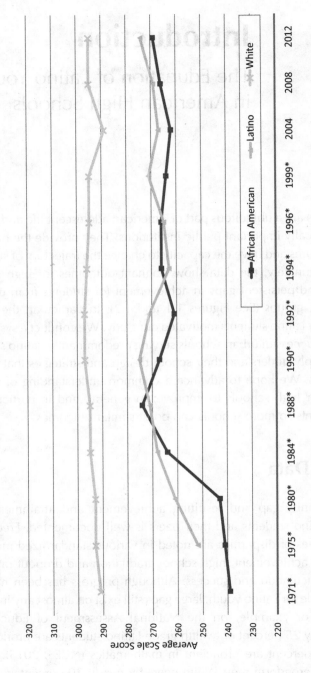

Figure 1.1 National Assessment of Educational Progress: Reading Scale Score, 17-year-olds

Source: National Center for Education Statistics, "The Nation's Report Card: Trends in Academic Progress 2012"

*Denotes previous assessment format

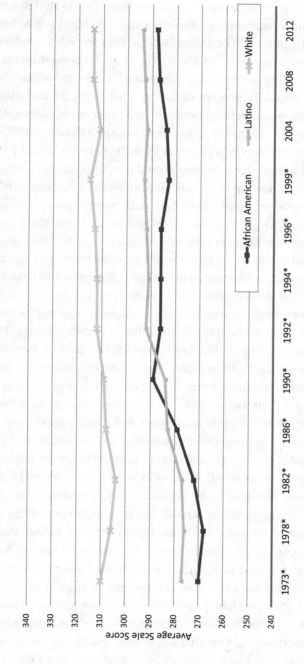

Figure 1.2 National Assessment of Educational Progress: Mathematics Scale Score, 17-year-olds

Source: National Center for Education Statistics, "The Nation's Report Card: Trends in Academic Progress 2012"

*Denotes previous assessment format

been increasing for all groups of students (with Latino students increasing the fastest thus narrowing the ethnicity gap), the Latino status dropout rate remains at 12 percent, compared to 5 percent for white students, and 1 percent for Asian students (NCES, 2016). As well, Latino students lag other groups in enrolling in four-year colleges and obtaining bachelor's degrees. As of 2016, about 21 percent of Latino adults ages 25 and older have a bachelor's degree or higher, compared to 32 percent of Blacks, 45 percent of Whites, and 53 percent of Asians (Pew Research Center, 2017). Although this represents tremendous progress from 2006 when only 11 percent of Latino's had a bachelor's degree, even the most prepared Latino students have trouble graduating from college (Carnevale & Fasules, 2017). Latino and White students with high SAT/ACT scores have similar college enrollment rates, a gap that has closed, but only 63 percent of these Latino students earn their degree compared to 78 percent of White students.

While all achievement gaps should generate moral outrage, the nation should be especially concerned about the achievement of Latino students, as they are the fastest growing demographic group. Currently, Latino students represent about a quarter of the public-school population and are expected to be the majority in 2050 (U.S. Census Bureau, Population Division, National Population Projections Tables, Table 6, Released 2008). In some states, like California and Texas, Latino students are already the majority. Latino students bring linguistic, social, and cultural assets to school, but the Civil Rights Data Collection documents many inequities in access and treatment that do not respect and capitalize on these strengths, thus contributing to the gaps in outcomes (U.S. Department of Education, OCR, 2014, 2016). For example, Latino students are more likely than their White peers to be enrolled in schools where more than 20 percent of teachers have not met state licensure requirements. And, 5 percent of teachers in largely White schools are new to the profession compared to 10 percent of teachers in largely Latino schools. Latino students also have less access to advanced courses and are less likely to be enrolled in gifted and talented programs. For example, 48 percent of U.S. high schools offer calculus, but only 33 percent of high schools with large Black and Latino student populations offer the course. Lastly, Latino students are disproportionately suspended from school, depriving them of learning opportunities. Research documents educators are more likely to identify Latino (and Black) students as "acting out" when they exhibit the same behaviors as their White peers. And, in addition to more disciplinary referrals, Latino students are likely to receive harsher consequences for similar offenses (Gregory, Skiba, & Noguera, 2010; Losen, 2015; Tennebaum & Ruck, 2007).

Identifying and Learning from Successful Urban Schools

Although the opportunity-, achievement-, and attainment-gap data are dire, there are schools that provide rich opportunities and achieve impressive academic results for Latino students. Since 2006, the National Center for Urban School Transformation (NCUST) at San Diego State University has been identifying, celebrating, and studying urban schools where children of color (including Latino students) achieve at levels equal to or greater than the average of all students in their state (Johnson, Perez, & Uline, 2012; Johnson, Uline, & Perez, 2017). Unfortunately, many educators do not realize that such high-performing, high-poverty, urban schools exist. Even if they are aware of high schools that generate strong results for Latino students, they might not have clear understandings about how leaders and educators in these schools have influenced these successes.

An exploratory case study of one award-winning NCUST high school that served a predominantly Latino population identified school practices that influenced better-than-average outcomes for Latino students. Specifically, the findings highlighted practices associated with curriculum, instruction, collaboration with families, relationships with students, and cultural competence as powerful tools to engage and support Latino students (Gonzalez, 2015). The research included in this book confirms and extends those findings by examining four additional NCUST award-winning high schools. Two schools serve a predominantly Latino population, while the other two schools have a majority of Latino students, but an overall diverse student population. Our goal was to understand each school deeply and to examine patterns and trends across schools that might point towards particularly powerful ideas for other educators to explore and apply in their schools. In the end, we noted key systems and structures in place in these schools and identified five key practices that were common across schools.

High school reform is replete with ideas. Sometimes it seems there is a new idea that is already gone or replaced by another new idea before it has had an opportunity to be implemented, refined and evaluated. This pattern suggests that high school educators want to improve their schools. Many educators are eager to pursue higher, more rigorous standards and equal outcomes for all students as are articulated in new state standards and accountability systems. It is this spirit that motivated us; we are not advocating a particular reform or program but are "looking under the hood" and examining perhaps the not-so- sexy stuff—every day practices that build strong schools, support teaching, and engage students.

We begin with a brief review of the literature on effective schools and the unique challenges facing schools that serve Latino students and emerging evidence of what works in these school contexts. The research broadly framed how we approached our study and how the field currently understands the problem and solutions to low academic achievement and postsecondary readiness in high schools. We attempt to add to this knowledge from educators who have done the hard work and have proven results with all students and Latino students in particular. Some say a few exceptions to the rule do not prove this work is possible and can be done at scale. We share their stories to ensure the hard-fought lessons they have learned are not isolated and can benefit more students. We describe our research methodology, how we selected the schools, and how we collected the data that led to the findings we share in subsequent chapters. Short profiles of each of the high schools are provided to introduce them to the reader and document why, in particular, they are worthy of study.

What Do We Know About Effective Schools?

There is a rich body of literature identifying practices associated with effective schools. Effective schools research began in earnest in the early 1970s after the publication of The Coleman Report, which postulated that schools had little impact on student achievement after socio-economic variables were considered (Coleman, 1966). However, the seemingly iron law of low income equating to low performance has always had exceptions. Researchers have vigorously studied and tried to identify the characteristics of these high-poverty/high-performing schools thus disproving the notion that "schools don't and can't make a difference" and that all students could master the core curriculum. The early round of this research identified a safe and orderly environment, high expectations, instructional leadership, focused mission, opportunity to learn, assessment of student progress and a positive home-school relationship as correlates of school effectiveness (Brookover & Lezotte, 1979; Edmonds, 1979; Lezotte, 1991; Rutter, 1979). While these studies were useful to the field, researchers were often critical of the findings suggesting they were overly simplistic and thinly supported by the data and small sample sizes (Purkey & Smith, 1983; Grady, Wayson, & Zirkel, 1989).

A new wave of effective schools or "beating the odds" studies emerged in the late 1990s and early 2000s with the advent of common standards and more robust student assessment systems (Marzano, 2003, 2005; Teddlie, Stringfield, Wimpelberg, & Kirby, 1989; The Charles A. Dana Center, 1999; The Education Trust, 1999, 2001; Togneri & Anderson, 2003). Two questions dominated the research: (1) whether and in what ways high-performing, high-poverty schools are organizationally different than low-performing, high-poverty schools and (2) what differentiates schools that improve from schools that do not (Bryk, Sebring, Allensworth, Luppescu, & Easton, 2010; Chenoweth, 2007, 2009; Chenoweth & Theokas, 2011; Leithwood, Louis, Anderson, & Wahlstrom, 2004; Parrett & Budge, 2012). While these studies affirmed much of the older research with more rigorous identification and analysis methods, they also attempted to deepen understanding of the correlates in ways that highlighted the salient aspects of school practices that influenced better student outcomes. For example, one study of over 60 high-performing urban schools focused specifically on the teaching practices employed in these schools, what set them apart from more typical schools and how they truly provided an "opportunity to learn" as articulated as essential in the original research (Johnson, Perez, & Uline, 2012). In these schools, students learned more because teachers planned and delivered quality first instruction, leading the majority of students to mastery the first time the concept was taught. The eight teaching practices that lead to mastery included, teacher clarity; introducing content logically, clearly and concisely; acquiring and responding to evidence of understanding; connecting with student interests, backgrounds, cultures, and prior knowledge; building student vocabulary; promoting successful practice; making students feel valued and capable; and leading students to love learning.

This research has been supplemented with a large body of quantitative literature examining the most powerful predictors of student achievement and asking not what works but, rather, what matters the most (Goodwin,

2010; Hattie, 2009; Marzano, 2001, 2003). For example, Hattie examined over 800 meta-analyses related to student achievement to determine which factors were most important by determining their degree of impact. He identified 250 factors that influence student-learning outcomes. While some of the factors, such as family resources, fell outside of the school's sphere of influence, those that were most likely to influence student learning fell squarely within the control of the school (e.g., teacher expectations, teacher collective efficacy, and feedback). Hattie's main point was that while many factors impact student achievement, teachers and principals should focus on employing those with the greatest evidence of impact.

Finally, the inter-relationships among correlates of school effectiveness became an area of focus. Most school variables when examined separately have an impact, as Hattie noted, but the real benefit comes when there is coherence and alignment across vision, goals, instructional strategies and educator actions. For example, leadership was identified as an "upstream" variable—one that influences all other variables but is not influenced by the other variables (Goodwin, 2010; Wallace Foundation, 2013). Leadership is essential to achieving coherence and critical mass, that is, ensuring effective practices are not isolated within individual classrooms or implemented poorly leading to no benefit for student learning. School leader responsibilities include setting the tone, culture and vision for the school, and managing the people, data, and processes in ways that foster instructional and school improvement (Chenoweth & Theokas, 2011, Wallace Foundation, 2013). Without effective leaders, urban schools are unlikely to change in the ways required or to improve and sustain the policies and practices that lead to positive student outcomes (Leithwood, Harris, & Strauss, 2010).

Johnson, Uline, and Perez (2017) note that critical mass is also achieved when school systems and processes work in concert with one another. They found that high-performing urban schools benefited from a "coherent educational improvement system" that helped develop, sustain, and improve culture, curricula, and instruction. Typical schools often have a multitude of disjointed systems and a profusion of programs that do not necessarily complement one another or provide clarity on the essential improvements that need to be made to better serve students. Leaders in high-performing urban schools confronted challenges, minimized barriers, and built coherence among the systems in their schools that led to exemplary outcomes. Instead of just a few classrooms or teachers producing results for students, high achievement was the norm in these schools. Outcomes of this coherent educational improvement system include, stakeholders feel valued and capable, there is a focus on specific concepts and skills, a clear assessment of mastery, improved initial instruction, and improved intervention and enrichment. In subsequent chapters, we will describe the structures, routines, policies, and norms that facilitate these outcomes to ensure Latino student success.

What Do We Know About Effective Schools For Latino Students?

Current research is focused less on understanding low-income students as a monolithic group and more on different ethnic groups' experiences and needs (Gandara, 2010; Nevarez & Rico, 2007). Latino students' needs may be different than Black or Filipino students' needs and further the Latino population, itself, is multifaceted. There are significant differences in immigrant status, language needs and culture as the population includes many different groups including Mexicans, Puerto Ricans, individuals from Latin or Central America, Cuba, and beyond. Research examining Latino students specifically has noted some specific trends that have implications for schools and their ability to close gaps between Latino students and their peers. First, Latino children have less access to preschool education than any other group and are more likely to come from homes where parents do not speak English well and where parental education is low. This results in many Latino students beginning school behind, on average, about six months behind their white peers. In addition, Latino students are slightly more likely than Black students to attend hyper segregated schools (Orfield & Frankenberg, 2008). Often, this isolates students from a robust college-going culture and perpetuates the lack of access to knowledge and experiences regarding broader societal expectations for student success. And, most importantly, schools have historically conceptualized Latino students' language and culture as disadvantages that hinder learning, rather than as assets to consider in teaching and learning. For example, policies at the federal, state and local level have often focused on English-only instruction, rather than supporting students to be bilingual and biliterate.

A number of programs have been successful in addressing some of the issues facing Latino children and youth by providing access to preschool

(Gormley, 2008), dual language or immersion programs (Gomez et al., 2005; Christian, Genesee, & Howard, 2004), dropout prevention efforts and college-going programs. Additionally, some schools have supported the success of Latino students by maintaining a significant number of bilingual administrators and professional staff to communicate with families (Lucas, Henze, & Donato, 1990), engaging Latino parents as resources to develop curricula (Berriz, 2002; Keenan, Willet, & Howard, 1993) and attending to students' English language proficiency and adapting classroom activities to maximize inclusion and participation (Herrell, 2000). These various strategies emphasize a common theme: when student identities are acknowledged and integrated into school operations, curriculum and instruction, Latino students can and do thrive (Au & Kawakami, 1994).

The body of research on improving outcomes for Latino students set the stage for our work. Yet, often, these other studies documented the success of a program or strategy in response to a perceived deficit or need. Instead, we were interested in learning how educators built coherent school designs that prepared all students to pursue postsecondary education and careers. Further, we focused on high schools. Where elementary and middle schools have shown some evidence of improving the achievement of Latino youngsters, high schools have been stubbornly resistant to reform and improvement. In high school, disengagement begins in earnest, students feel "pushed" out and not welcomed into the intellectual community, and the gap between aspirations and attainment grows. How do high schools build and support the postsecondary aspirations of a variety of students, at different achievement levels, and with different levels of English proficiency? We sought to collect and raise up the voices of educators, students, and families who have created and experienced schools that close gaps between Latino students and their peers. We describe our methodology below.

Study Methodology

The research reported here is part of an ongoing effort by the National Center for Urban School Transformation (NCUST) to learn from highly effective urban schools. Over the past decade, NCUST has visited nearly 150 outstanding urban elementary, middle, and high schools to learn about the practices, policies and systems they employ to get all demographic groups of students to achieve at or above state averages on multiple indicators of academic success. We have distilled our findings in two prior books, *Teaching Practices from America's Best Urban Schools* and *Leadership in America's Best Urban Schools*.

Over the years, fewer high schools (than elementary or middle schools) have met our criteria and earned our award (see Table 1.1 for award criteria). Through this study, we focused upon high-performing high schools to get a better sense of the challenges they faced and how they overcame them. We specifically examined high-performing high schools that served a predominantly Latino population, because few U.S. high schools generate strong evidence of postsecondary readiness for Latino students, and these schools address important issues related to language and culture in ways that deserve special attention.

Table 1.1 America's Best Urban Schools Award Criteria

Urban Location:	The school must be located in a metropolitan area with 50,000 or more residents.
Non-Selective Admissions:	In general, the school may not require students to meet academic criteria in order to attain or retain admission. Schools may house programs (e.g., programs for students identified as gifted or talented) that admit children from beyond the school's attendance area through selective admissions if fewer than 10 percent of the school's students are enrolled through selective admissions.
Low-Income Eligibility:	At least 40 percent of the students must have met the states low-income eligibility criteria (typically free and reduced-price lunch).
High Rates of Academic Proficiency for Every Racial/ Ethnic Group:	The school must indicate the percentage of students from each racial/ethnic group who achieved academic proficiency. The school may be eligible to compete only if, in at least two academic subjects, the percentage of students proficient in each racial/ethnic group exceeds the average of all schools in the state.
Evidence of High Achievement for English Learners:	If more than 20 students are identified as English learners, the school must provide the number and percent of students who progressed to the next level on the state English assessment. As well, the school must indicate the percentage of English learners that achieved proficiency on state assessments.

continued . . .

Table 1.1 Continued

Evidence of High Achievement for Students with Disabilities:	The school must indicate the percentage of students with disabilities that achieved proficiency on state assessments.
Low Rates of Out-of-School Suspension:	For every demographic group served, with an enrollment greater than 20, the total number of student days lost to suspensions must be less than the total number of students enrolled.
High Attendance Rates:	The school must have evidence to indicate that the average student attendance rate exceeded 95% for each of the past two academic years.
Low Rates of Teacher Absence:	Schools must indicate the percentage of teachers who were absent more than 10 days. The rate must not exceed the national average.
Percentage of First-Year High School Students Advancing to the Second Year:	Each high school must present the number and percentage of their first-year students who earned sufficient credit to be promoted to second-year status.
Percentage of Students Earning College Credit or Participating in Advanced Placement Courses during High School:	Each school must present evidence of the number and percentage of students who earned college credit in the prior year. Also, each applicant must present evidence of the number and percentage of students who participated in advanced placement or international baccalaureate courses; the number and percentage who took advanced placement or international baccalaureate assessments; and the number and percentage who received passing scores. Schools also provide average SAT/ACT scores.
High Graduation Rates:	Each high school must present the latest four-year adjusted cohort graduation rate (as defined by the U.S. Department of Education) for every racial/ethnic group of students.
Schools must also respond to several open-ended questions that ask for evidence of rigorous curricula, engaging and effective instruction, a positive school culture, student engagement in extracurricular activities, excellence in Science, Technology, Engineering, and Mathematics education (STEM), and describe what efforts the school is making to ensure students are successful in subsequent school levels.	

Research Design

We employed a multi-site case study design (Yin, 1994). This method allowed for the holistic and meaningful consideration of various constructs in the investigation of organizational systems, culture and processes that led to Latino student success in high school. Prior research conducted by NCUST suggested critical constructs to study including teacher–student relationships, cultural awareness and inclusion in learning, and leadership support for learning. We realize we cannot say with certainty what factors contributed to these schools' success, but the case study approach allowed us to collect practical, detailed information about what experienced and successful educators believed led to educational successes and how they pursued those actions.

At each of the four schools, key stakeholders (superintendents, principals, administrators, teachers, students, staff, and parents) were selected to provide information concerning their roles, experiences, beliefs and perceptions about school practices and why Latino students were succeeding at their school and not at other similar schools. Perspectives were collected through semi-structured interviews and focus groups and analyzed to identify the most salient themes within and across stakeholder groups. A semi-structured approach was selected to define general areas to be explored, based on prior research, but also to allow the questioning or responses to diverge in order to pursue an idea or response in more detail that was relevant to the school's success. One-on-one interviews were conducted with school leaders to explore constructs and their implementation more deeply, while focus groups were conducted with stakeholder groups to stimulate discussion among group members, ensuring comprehensive coverage of ideas and revealing divergent thinking amongst group members with similar roles and responsibilities.

In addition, two additional qualitative data-collection methods—observation and document analysis—were employed to provide converging lines of inquiry and to enhance the power of the case study findings and conclusions. School and classroom observations allowed us to document application of school practices and policies and to collect specific examples of practices including, for example, professional learning communities and instructional methods. Observations were used not only to validate the information educators shared in interviews, but also to provide examples that helped illustrate and differentiate oft-referenced concepts in education such as data use, collaboration, or the use of questions in class discussions. Artifact collection and document analysis provided additional evidence and examples that brought concepts discussed in interviews and focus groups to life. For example, we collected bell schedules, agendas from planning meetings, and professional development topics.

The raw interview data were organized by school and also by constituent (e.g., students) across cases. Our goal was to deeply understand each individual school, but also to look for themes across schools. Interview data, focus-group data, and field notes were transcribed, and all data, including artifacts and observations, were coded by multiple researchers to identify the themes distilled in this book.

High School Sample

Four high schools from the NCUST America's Best Urban Schools (ABUS) Award database were selected as the primary units of study (brief profiles of each of the schools follow). Each had won the ABUS award between 2014 and 2017. They are located in three different states (California, Texas, and Massachusetts) with different state policy and local contexts. Schools ranged in size from approximately 500 to 2,000 for student enrollment and all were located in urban areas. Each school served a large proportion of Latino students (range: 54–99 percent), students learning English (range: 14–21 percent), students with a first language that was not English, and economically disadvantaged students (range: 59–100 percent). Each state utilized different economic disadvantage indicators, but generally, the schools were considered to be serving low-income communities and dealing with the attendant challenges. We selected schools that served an almost all Latino student population as well as schools with more diverse populations to see if the strategies varied based on the size of the Latino student population. Our goal was to select schools that were serving the local neighborhood population and were exceeding state expectations and averages for all student groups. In addition, all schools met the specific attendance, behavioral (i.e., suspensions/discipline), academic, and graduation eligibility criteria established to certify it as one of America's Best Urban Schools (see Table 1.2 for individual school data).

Table 1.2 Study Schools

	Eastlake HS	O'Farrell HS	Pace HS	Revere HS
Location	TX	CA	TX	MA
Number Students	2,079	500	2,074	1,991
Asian		19%		6%
African American	2%	19%		4%
Latino	94%	54%	99%	56%
White	3%	2%		31%
Economically Disadvantaged	69%	74%	100%	59%
English Learners	13%	21%	14%	16%

High School Visits

Beyond the initial visit associated with NCUST's America's Best Urban Schools Award process, where five or more staff visited and collected information about the school, we visited each school for two days in the Spring of 2017. During each visit, we interviewed faculty, staff, parents, and students; observed classrooms, special events, and staff meetings; and collected essential artifacts. The number of staff interviewed varied due to high school size and structure with different numbers of administrators, teachers and students. Our goal was to include the entire leadership team and a representative number of faculty from each grade and department. As well, we interviewed 15–25 students including both male and female Latino students with diverse educational profiles, 5–10 Latino parents at each school and diverse groups of support staff based on school recommendations. For example, this group may include, school security, facilities staff, food service workers, front office staff, counselors, parent coordinators, or office staff. We also observed in classrooms during regular instruction and attended various staff meetings (e.g., all school, grade level collaboration meetings). While observing, we conducted various informal interviews with staff and students to learn more about their roles and experiences at the school.

School Profiles

Eastlake High School

Eastlake High School, in El Paso County, Texas is one of 47 schools in the Socorro Independent School District. The district serves more than 46,000 students on El Paso's east side. Eastlake opened in August 2010 and was the fifth of six traditional, comprehensive high schools. Socorro is a rapidly growing district that also includes four specialty early college high school campuses. Eastlake graduated its first class in 2014 and has been under the leadership of principal Gilbert Martinez since 2012, although he started at the school when it first opened its doors. Eastlake serves about 2,070 students, with the majority being Latino (94 percent). Eastlake sits right on the border of Mexico, but also serves students from the local military base Fort Bliss. About 70 percent of students are classified as economically disadvantaged, 39 percent at risk and 14 percent are considered English learners. Eastlake "met standard" in 2016 as defined by the Texas Education Agency and exceeded expectations on the four performance indices: student performance, student progress, closing performance gaps, and postsecondary readiness. As well, Eastlake earned six of seven state distinctions. Student academic achievement scores continue to rise in all subject areas, with targeted focus being placed on English I to help improve reading comprehension and writing.

In addition to their academic awards and multiple extracurricular opportunities and accomplishments, Eastlake is a very welcoming school focused on providing students with "endless opportunities," (the district's motto). The school facility is large and expansive, offering extensive opportunities from a veterinary clinic, to an industrial kitchen, to multiple rooms for band, dance, and art. In 2016, Eastlake students participated on study trips to Beijing, Italy, and Spain. They follow a hybrid, year-round calendar with a two-week intercession in the fall and spring and one month in the summer for summer school that further allows for intervention and enrichment. Student learning and preparation for postsecondary is the priority. According to the students at Eastlake, "Teachers go overboard to help you." And, "A lot of the teachers are really enthusiastic about the subject they teach, which helps a lot with learning the class." And, "They will adjust their schedule for you. So, if you can't make it at a certain time, they'll come in early or they will come after school to help you."

The O'Farrell High School

The O'Farrell High School is located in San Diego, CA and serves about 500 students in grades 9–12. The school converted to a charter school in the fall of 1994 with a seventh grade cohort. Today, O'Farrell serves kindergarten through twelfth grade students with the mission of providing a multi-cultural, linguistically, and racially diverse learning environment in which students experience educational equity and are encouraged to celebrate their own individuality. All students, upon graduation, are expected to have acquired the fundamental tools and skills to move seamlessly on to the college of their choice. School-wide decisions are made by a board of directors that meets once a month and consists of teacher, parent, and community representatives. In addition to a super-intendent, each school—elementary, middle and high—has its own principal to oversee the curriculum and operations of the school. Mr. Rainey has been principal of the high school since they rolled out their first cohort that graduated in 2016.

The high school population is diverse, 54 percent Latino, 19 percent African American, 19 percent Asian, and 2 percent White. Seventy-four percent of students are economically disadvantaged and 21 percent are English learners. Student performance on English and mathematics exams exceed the state average by 10 percentage points in math and by nearly 20 percentage points in reading. O'Farrell's "secret sauce," Homebase, a daily period for a small group of students and a teacher that remain together through high school, will be discussed in relation to the core practices in the following chapters, but according to Mr. Rainey, "It is our first way of making sure every kid is known and loved. And then beyond that, every teacher works on their teacher–student relationships in their classrooms, so that there aren't any cracks for kids to fall through." The school is structured around relationships, high standards and character development. All of the students in the first graduating class were accepted to college, their goal.

Pace Early College High School

"Powerful" was the one word Principal Longoria used to describe her school, Pace Early College High School, a high school in the Brownsville Independent School District in Brownsville, TX. Brownsville sits right on the border of Mexico, with many students coming daily from Mexico to attend school or living with a 'tutora' in the U.S. during the school week. The school district serves nearly 50,000 students on 58 different campuses and has won many accolades including the Broad Prize for Urban Education in 2008. More recently, Brownsville was found to lead the nation on the education equality index developed by Education Cities and Great Schools; students from low-income families in Brownsville perform just as well or better on state standardized math and reading tests than their more advantaged peers in 500 schools across the country.

Pace serves over 2,000 students, all of whom are classified as economically disadvantaged. Ninety-nine percent are Latino and 14 percent are English learners. Like Eastlake, the school "met standard" for the state of Texas in 2016; exceeded all four, performance indicators; and earned six of seven possible distinctions. They far exceeded state averages in all subject areas with the exception of English, a challenge that Principal Rose Longoria is determined to meet. When talking with students about what they would like to change at their school, they could not think of anything. When pressed, they agreed they did like the old marquee they have out in front of the school. Pace is an older facility, and they felt it did not match the quality and pride they have in their school. One teacher compared Pace to other campuses she had worked on and said,

> This is very a different environment that has been created here. It's very unique; it's very special. It doesn't feel like this at other schools that serve the same type of students that we do. It's usually the teachers are there to teach and then once done with their lesson, they go home. Whereas here, you can go into various hallways and you hear, "Oh hey, how was your baseball game?" or "How was your basketball game?" and maybe that student is not in their class any longer. But we keep up with what's going on, I think that that is a testament to the type of school climate that has been created here. And in the end, I think that allows our students to feel more comfortable and be more willing to work or do projects in your class because they know that we're not sitting here just trying to be that mundane, robotic-type of teacher. We're here because, you know, we love to teach but we value and we love our students.

Revere High School

Dr. Lourenco Garcia leads Revere High School in Revere, MA, just five miles north of downtown Boston. One hundred percent of students complete the MassCore—the recommended, rigorous course of study (based on standards in Massachusetts's curriculum frameworks) that aligns high school coursework with college and career expectations. Revere High School serves a diverse population of nearly 2,000 including Latino (56 percent), White (31 percent), Asian (6 percent), and African American (4 percent) students. Moreover, 59 percent of the student population is considered high needs; 80 percent receive free and reduced-price lunch. As well, approximately 60 percent of students do not speak English as their first language, and 16 percent remain classified as English language learners. The district is relatively small with 11 schools serving almost 7,500 students. Revere is the main high school, with one smaller alternative high school that serves about 130 students. A unique feature of RHS is the continuity of their mission. The school has followed a path of rigor, relevance, relationships and resilience for a number of years and across different principals, with the unequivocal support of district leadership. This has allowed Revere to deepen its practices each year and also innovate to continually improve and better meet the needs of students. As of 2014, 80 percent of the school's graduates matriculate into college. The school had about a one percent dropout rate. Around 2008 the rate of students attending tertiary education was 67 percent and the dropout rate was almost 9 percent.

When talking with teachers about the diverse student population and Latino students in particular, one teacher captured the essence of Revere,

> I think we work really hard at trying to, in addition to things like cultural competency, have a really big part of the conversation around here be about teaching with high expectations for all students. So, we try not to have a perception of a student when they walk into the room. We try to focus on what is this individual student able to do? What are their strengths? What are their weaknesses? How do we speak to their strengths? How can we speak to their weaknesses? And, the administration is really open-minded about the kind of text that we can bring into the classroom

and making sure that we find ways to appeal to students by supplementing, anchor texts that are central to the unit with supplemental readings or supplemental film clips or supplemental poetry or songs. We're given the leeway to be as creative as we can be, to engage as many students as we can. It's by no means perfect, I mean, we're working on our cultural competency because, you know, there's still a lot of work to be done. But we're working really hard to investigate those things. We have teachers that are in pilot groups that are experimenting within their own classrooms to the extent that they are comfortable doing it, and we're reporting back to administration and we're looking at success that we're having and we're trying to stick with the things that we think we are working for all students and leaving behind the stuff that we think doesn't really add to our work.

Conclusion

We set out to understand how effective, urban high schools, their leaders and staff improve learning outcomes for all students, and Latino students, in particular. Some of our research questions included: What goals, characteristics, programs, and systems were shared across schools? Which were different and why? How did students and staff experience these schools? What did student and staff experiences suggest about how they operated? We were able to distill the key patterns and themes in the data down to five practices. Each chapter describes in detail a core element of their school design and the final chapter summarizes the five key practices we identified as essential for their success.

These schools are important because they face many of the same challenges encountered by urban high schools across the United States; yet, they achieve remarkable results for all students, and especially Latino students. Their results exceed statewide averages on multiple indicators of performance and their results are often considerably better than neighboring high schools serving similar populations, with similar challenges and high schools serving much more advantaged populations. Through our study of these impressive schools, we learned that there is reason to be hopeful for the education of Latino youth in America's urban high schools.

Educators can, in collaboration with their communities, create vibrant learning environments that prepare all students to succeed in postsecondary learning opportunities and careers. The following chapters describe how it can be done.

References

Au, K. H., & Kawakami, A. J. (1994). Cultural congruence in instruction. In E. R. Hollins, J. E. King; & W. C. Hayman (Eds.), *Teaching diverse populations*. New York: SUNY Press.

Berriz, B. R. (2002). Connecting classroom and community through the arts and oral narrative. In Z. F. Beykont (Ed.), *The power of culture: Teaching across language difference*. Cambridge, MA: Harvard Education Publishing Group.

Brookover, W. B., & Lezotte, L.W. (1979). *Changes in school characteristics coinci- dent with changes in student achievement* (Occasional Paper No. 17). East Lansing, MI: Michigan State University, East Lansing Institute for Research in Teaching.

Bryk, A., Sebring, P. B., Allensworth, E., Luppescu, S., & Easton, J. O. (2010). *Organizing schools to improve: Lessons from Chicago*. Chicago, IL: Chicago University Press.

Carnevale, A., & Fasules, M. (2017). *Latino Education and economic progress: Running faster but still behind*. Washington, DC: Georgetown University, Center on Education and the Workforce.

Charles A. Dana Center. (1999). *Hope for urban education: A study of nine high-performing, high poverty urban elementary schools*. University of Texas at Austin: Charles A. Dana Center and Washington, DC: U.S. Department of Education, Planning and Evaluation Service.

Chenoweth, K. (2007). *It's being done: Academic success in unexpected schools*. Cambridge, MA: Harvard Education Press.

Chenoweth, K. (2009). *How it's being done: Academic success in unexpected schools*. Cambridge, MA: Harvard Education Press.

Chenoweth, K., & Theokas, C. (2011). *Getting it done: Leading academic success in unexpected Schools*. Cambridge, MA: Harvard Education Press.

Christian, D., Genesee, F. K., and Howard, L. (2004). *Project 1.2 two-way immersion: Final progress report*. Santa Cruz, CA, and Washington, DC: Center for Research on Education, Diversity & Excellence.

Coleman, J. (1966). *Equality of educational opportunity*. Washington, DC: U.S. Government Printing Office.

Edmonds, R. (1979). Effective schools for the urban poor. *Educational Leadership*, *37*, 15–24.

The Education Trust (1999). *Dispelling the myth: High poverty schools exceeding expectations*. Report of the Education Trust in cooperation with the Council of Chief State School Officers and partially funded by the U.S. Department of Education, Washington, DC, 2001.

The Education Trust (2001). Dispelling the myth revisited: Preliminary findings from a nationwide analysis of "high-flying" schools. Washington, DC: The Education Trust.

Gándara, P. (2010). The Latino education crisis. *Educational Leadership*, *67*(5), 24–30.

Gándara, P., & Contreras, F. (2009). *The Latino education crisis: The consequences of failed social policies*. Cambridge, MA: Harvard University Press.

Gregory, A., Skiba, R. J., & Noguera, P. (2010). The achievement gap and the discipline gap: Two sides of the same coin? *Educational Researcher*, *39*(1), 59–68.

Gómez, L., Freeman, D., & Freeman, Y. (2005). Dual language education: A 50-50 model. *Bilingual Research Journal*, *29*(1), 145–64.

Gonzalez, M. L. (2015). *Latino males and academic achievement*. Doctoral dissertation, San Diego State University.

Goodwin, B. (2010). *Changing the odds for student success: What matters most*. Denver, CO: Mid-continent Research for Education and Learning (McREL).

Gormley, W. (2008). The effects of Oklahoma's pre-k program on Hispanic children. *Social Science Quarterly*, *89*, 916–36.

Grady, M. L, Wayson W.W., & Zirkel, P. A. (1989). *A review of effective schools research as it relates to effective principals*. UCEA Monograph Series. Tempe, AZ: University Council of Educational Administration.

Hattie, J. (2009). *Visible Learning*. London: Routledge.

Herrell, A. L. (2000). *Fifty strategies for teaching English language learners*. Upper Saddle River, NJ: Prentice-Hall.

Johnson, J. F., Perez, L. G., & Uline, C. L. (2012). *Teaching practices from America's best urban schools: A guide for school and classroom leaders*. New York: Routledge.

Johnson, J. F., Uline, C. L., & Perez, L. G. (2017). *Leadership in America's best urban schools*. New York: Routledge.

Keenan, J. W., Willet, U., and Solsken, J. (1993). Constructing an urban village: School/home collaboration in a multicultural classroom. *Language Arts, 70*(3), 204–14.

Leithwood, K., Harris, A., & Strauss, T. (2010). *Leading school turnaround: How successful leaders transform low-performing schools*. San Francisco, CA: John Wiley and Sons.

Lezotte, L. W. (1991). *Correlates of effective schools: The first and second generation*. Okemos, MI: Effective Schools Products.

Lopez, G. R. (2001). The value of hard work: Lessons on parent involvement from an (im)migrant household. *Harvard Educational Review, 71*, 416–37.

Losen, D. (2015). Security measures and discipline in American high schools. In Daniel J. Losen, Jeremy D. Finn, & Timothy J. Servoss (Eds.), *Closing the school discipline gap: Equitable remedies for excessive exclusion*. New York: Teachers College Press.

Lucas, T., Henze, R., and Donato, R. (1990). Promoting the success of Latino language majority-minority students. *Harvard Educational Review, 60*(3), *315–40*.

Marzano, R. J. (2001). *Classroom instruction that works*. Alexandria, VA: ASCD.

Marzano, R. J. (2003). *What works in schools: Translating research into action*. Alexandria, VA: ASCD.

Marzano, R. J., Waters, T., & McNulty, B. A. (2005). *School leadership that works: From research to results*. Alexandria, VA: ASCD.

National Center for Education Statistics (NCES). (2015). *The condition of education, 2015*. Washington, DC: U.S. Government Printing Office.

National Center for Education Statistics (NCES). (2016). *The digest of education statistics 2016*. Washington, DC: U.S. Government Printing Office.

Nevarez, C., & Rico, T. (2007). *Latino education: A synthesis of recurring recommendations and solutions in P-16 education*. Washington, DC: The College Board.

Orfield, G., & Frankenberg, E. (2008). *The last have become first: Rural and small town America lead the way of desegregation*. Los Angeles, CA: UCLA Civil Rights Project/Proyecto Derechez Civiles.

Parrett, W. H., & Budge, K. (2012). *Turning high-poverty schools into high-performing schools*. ASCD: Alexandria, VA.

Pew Research Center. (2009). *Between two worlds: How young Latinos come of age in America*. Washington, DC: Pew Research Center.

Pew Research Center. (2016). *Five facts about Latinos and education*. Washington, DC: Pew Research Center.

Pew Research Center. (2017). *More Hispanic high school graduates are enrolling in college*. Washington, DC: Pew Research Center.

Purkey, S. C., & Smith, M. S. (1983). Effective schools: A review. *The Elementary School Journal, 83*(4), 427–52.

Rutter, M. (1979). *Fifteen thousand hours*. Cambridge, MA: Harvard University Press.

Suarez-Orozco, C., & Suarez-Orozco, M. M. (1995). *Transformations: Immigration, family life, achievement motivation among Latino adolescents*. Stanford, CA: Stanford University Press.

Teddlie, C., Stringfield, S., Wimpelberg, R., & Kirby, P. (1989). Contextual differences in models for effective schooling in the USA. In *School Effectiveness and School Improvement, Swets et Zeitlinger, Amsterdam*, 117–30.

Togneri, W., & Anderson, S. E. (2003). How high poverty districts improve. *Leadership, 33*(1), 12–16.

Tenenbaum H., & Ruck, M. (2007). Are teachers' expectations different for racial minority than for European American students? A meta-analysis. *Journal of Educational Psychology, 99*(2), 253–73.

U.S. Census Bureau. (2008). Population Division, National Population Projections Tables, Table 6. Released 2008. Washington DC.

U.S. Census Bureau. (2014). October current population survey. Washington DC.

U.S. Department of Education Office for Civil Rights. (2014). Civil rights data collection data snapshot: College and career readiness. Washington DC.

U.S. Department of Education Office for Civil Rights. (2016). 2013–2014 Civil rights data collection: A first look. Washington DC.

Wallace Foundation. (2013). *The school principal as leader: Guiding schools to better teaching and learning.* New York: The Wallace Foundation.

Yin, R. (1994). *Case study research: Design and methods.* Beverly Hills, CA: SAGE Publications.

2 | Promoting Commitment and Shared Responsibility

Mr. Martinez's motto is "Together, we're better." He repeats it quite often. He'll come into a room and say, 'I'm good. You're good, but together, we're better.' I think that is the epitome of what goes on here at Eastlake. We're good individually. As a coach, this is something I preach to my kids. Individually, you have great talent, but the sum of your efforts will never amount to the sum of our collective efforts. And collectively, we are working so hard not only for our kids to be successful, but to thrive, to thrive not only in this setting but to thrive beyond here. So, working together, we can better prepare them for a great future.

—Assistant Principal, Eastlake High School

Decades of education research have clearly documented the impact of leadership on student achievement. In fact, principal leadership is second only to classroom instruction among all of the school-related factors that affect student learning (Leithwood, Louis, Anderson, & Wahlstrom, 2004; Leithwood, Harris, & Strauss, 2010; Marzano, Waters, & McNulty, 2005; Waters, Marzano, & McNulty, 2003). Further, the impact of leadership appears strongest in schools that serve low-income communities (Leithwood, Louis, Anderson, & Wahlstrom, 2004). High-performing, high-poverty schools demand effective leaders who can work through the challenges associated with change and create a team committed to a shared goal (Chenoweth & Theokas, 2012; Johnson, Uline, & Perez, 2017).

The beliefs, behaviors, and actions of effective principals have been well documented, and, we know that effective principals leave nothing to chance. One way that principals ensure essential priorities are addressed routinely and productively is by creating a high-functioning administrative or leadership team to lead the everyday work of the school and to communicate and model priorities. This is particularly important in large, comprehensive high schools with hundreds of students who have four short years to accumulate the knowledge, skills, and abilities to be ready for postsecondary education and work. No amount of hours, passion, or commitment of a single individual can accomplish this daunting task. Principals in the four high schools we studied relied heavily on other administrators and educators to help enact their vision of excellence for all students. And, they articulated clear roles and expectations for every administrator (and staff member) in ways that addressed issues central to improving learning results. This vision, clarity, and leadership created a very strong and effective school community focused on progress and success for all groups of students. Nothing is left to chance and no student is left behind. Stakeholders perceived a shared commitment and responsibility for student outcomes. As a student in one of the schools explained:

> They don't want to see anybody being left behind. Like they want to help you so that everybody is up there at the same level. They want to push you to do the best that you can and maybe even more than that.

Shaping a Vision of Academic Success for All Students

First and foremost, leaders in these schools shared a vision that was based on high standards. At a minimum, they expected their students to meet or exceed state standards. Mastery was the driver of instruction to ensure each and every student would be ready and prepared to pursue his or her dreams upon graduation. They believed in their students and as one teacher said, "Success is the standard on our campus; excelling is the standard. We set that standard and we don't let them believe they can't achieve." Some experienced teachers went further to note that they heard that same success standard articulated at other schools, but in practice it was not implemented. They reflected, it is easy to say you have high standards, but much more difficult to match your practices to that standard. And, in the face of challenges stay committed to that goal. At these four high schools, the bar is not lowered, they refuse to give up on students, they "double down" and figure out what support is needed and they expect students to meet them halfway.

In later chapters, we discuss how the vision of success was clearly embedded in these schools' cultures, systems and routines. Here, we want to share how the principals took on the challenge of establishing the school vision and distributing leadership among their teams to achieve the goal of excellence for each and every student. *Having an important purpose was the first key practice we identified*. It set the stage for the school design and focus on student interests and needs. The principals are the first ones to credit their teams with their students' success. They humbly refuse recognition and praise, but we think it is important to share where they started, how they created the vision, communicated it and then how the vision manifests itself in the daily work/life of the school. Ultimately, the principals knew it was their responsibility to help members of the school community achieve unity of purpose. The clear and important purpose guided the work and was only able to be accomplished by a team who believed it was possible and shared responsibility for accomplishing it. *Shared ownership and leadership for the school vision and goals was also a key practice in the school's success*. If the vision was at the center of school operations, the team surrounded and encompassed it to ensure its success.

School Mottos that Engage Staff and Students and Articulate a Purpose

When we visited each high school, we felt an immediate clarity of purpose. We noticed each school had a motto or set of values that rallied both staff and students. The mottos were not merely about individual academic success. Instead, the mottos articulated and promoted a community commitment to every student in attendance. These mottos represented the true ethos of the school and could be seen and felt in little interactions, as well as in big choices and decisions made by each school. These mottos and their implicit values (see Table 2.1) were the brand of the school and something everyone was proud of and happy to talk about. It was the larger purpose everyone was committed to that had personal meaning and relevance for students and staff alike.

Generally, we would argue that there is no power in a phrase hanging on the wall; too often schools spend lots of time coming up with their

Table 2.1 School Mottos

School	Motto
Eastlake High School	Together, we are better.
The O'Farrell High School	The Falcon Way: Focus, Attitude, Leadership, Citizenship, Organization and Non-Violence
Revere High School	The Four Rs: Rigor, Relationships, Relevance and Resiliency
Pace Early College High School	Educate Students, Graduate Leaders, Empower Communities

vision statement only to post it on the wall and never think about it again. We have all experienced asking school faculty their vision and either having someone struggle to come up with the posted vision or alternatively not be able to articulate the purpose they collectively as a school were working toward. At these four schools, their mottos are repeated often and have become a part of the belief system of students and adults at the schools. The mottos strengthened a sense of community and cemented a connection to the goal of postsecondary readiness. Students and staff looked upon the mottos with humor, commitment, belief, and pride, often despite themselves. Across all stakeholders group, the motto would inevitably come up in conversation. For example, a student at O'Farrell said,

> My favorite thing about school is that, it might be cheesy, we're all like a family and I feel like if I have a problem or whatever, I could just go to any teacher, to be honest, or any one of my classmates. It's the Falcon Way.

Or, as a teacher at Revere said, "As corny as it sounds, we call it The Four R's now. I think those four things really do exemplify the teachers in this schools." And, when talking with a group of students at Pace about their school, one student was sharing that they weren't the stereotype people believed about Mexicans, and one student began saying, "Every day, we . . ." and before she could finish her thought, the whole group chimed in and said, "Educate students, graduate leaders, and empower the community!"

These mottos indicate that these schools do not narrowly define the success of their students. True, they want their students to be academically successful, but they have big aspirations for their students that far exceed state test results. Initially, we selected these schools for study because of their very high test results, but their goals for their students go well beyond this. They truly take to heart that they are preparing the next generation and that their students are part of the larger community they all share.

Opportunities and Challenges in Establishing the Vision

The principals in these high schools had different opportunities and challenges related to establishing the school vision and developing a team to support continuous improvement toward the school goals. We noted some striking similarities in beliefs and outcomes.

Eastlake High School

Eastlake was a new school built to serve a rapidly growing community. The school population is diverse economically serving some of the lowest income areas of El Paso, while also drawing from new subdivisions with larger homes and middle-income families and also children of military personnel at nearby Fort Bliss. Mr. Martinez was adamant that Eastlake would "never be a traditional high school." By this, he meant, he did not want the school to have cliques; he wanted a cohesive, small community feel that was student-centered and based on caring relationships and a commitment to supporting one another. He insisted the school would be welcoming to everyone and staff would know all the students and families. As well as this, they would offer as many opportunities as possible to students, ensuring everyone had a place and they would have high expectations for all students.

Eastlake took that challenge associated with size to heart and as they added grades each year, Mr. Martinez was determined that all new staff would understand that commitment. He believes it is a mindset and talks about it with new staff and creates opportunities to model it to staff.

Personally, he has monthly meetings with three or four student representatives from each grade who serve on the principal's advisory committee (PAC). He also meets regularly with the ambassadors' club (club and team leaders across the campus) to hear the students' perspective on priorities and needs of the student body. For example, the school was built with facilities for industrial trades; however, students were not interested in signing up for these courses and pathways. So, Mr. Martinez asked the students why they weren't choosing those classes and they told him they wanted law and criminal justice—so they changed the space. Mr. Martinez reflected, "They are going to tell you what they want, and you've got to listen. You've got to be able to respond. Because, they will hold you accountable." As well, he discusses district initiatives with the students to learn their ideas on how to pursue those initiatives at Eastlake. Safety is one of the current initiatives and when Mr. Martinez discussed it with his students, they were not concerned about bullying or social media on their campus, but they did feel like suicide was a concern and wanted him to address it. Mr. Martinez's question to the students was, "How? What would you all want to hear?"

He also hosts either coffee or dinner with the principal each month for the families. The meetings alternate to ensure that everyone who wishes to attend can. Dinner meetings are held in the school "restaurant." Students prepare and serve the meal with the supervision of Chef Robeles to showcase the students and program. These meetings are one way Mr. Martinez communicates and models the importance of everyone knowing and valuing the students and families. He is not an authoritarian leader who tells others to "do it my way," but rather, acts as if he believes that all stakeholders have valuable perspectives and he prioritizes open communication.

One way the administrative team operationalizes the commitment to know and value students is by eating lunch in the cafeteria every day with the students. Diverse groups of students sit together and hang out; it was not uncommon for students who participated in very different types of activities to sit together. As well, administrators and guests also sat with students. During our visit, students welcomed us to sit with them. They both answered our questions and asked us questions about our work and ourselves. The administration also celebrated student and staff accomplishments during morning announcements, when dropping into classrooms, and when they saw students and staff in the hallways.

Similarly, staff also held students accountable if their behavior did not meet their expectations. They were known to ask students about a choice they made by saying, "How was this taking care of yourself? How was this taking care of your school? How was this taking care of each other?" It was important for staff to use both positive and negative opportunities to connect students to the school campus expectations. Celebrations are extremely important, but so are direct conversations when expectations are not being met.

Students at Eastlake reflected that their school lacked the long-established athletic traditions that neighboring high schools boasted. This deficiency, however, was more than remedied by what students referred to as their feeling that they were part of a family or team. Students claimed they felt part of a family that believed in them. When asked what they wanted us to remember about their school, the students said Eastlake was a diverse community that brings lots of different people and cultures together who support one another.

Students at Revere said almost the same thing about their school.

> ... How diverse it is. How welcoming. All the students and the teachers—everyone—tries to help you with your problems. They don't discriminate. They don't criticize us. It's a very welcoming place. It's like a second home for the students, or better yet, home for some kids.

The idea of being a family was a common theme among all stakeholders across schools. Everyone at Eastlake felt part of the family and knew their role in helping to make the school welcoming, collaborative and excellent. They valued everyone else's role and contribution to the school, recognizing they needed each other to do their jobs better. For example, the custodial staff shared that they believed the school was the students' second home and they felt responsible for keeping it tidy, but they also expected the students to do the same. "And, we always treat the students with respect, that's the biggest one. Treat the student with respect. Treat them as family."

The family liaison coordinator relied on the facility and food service staff to help her set up events and meetings. Similarly, security was there to keep things safe, but they also saw themselves as mentors for the students and a resource to support teachers, so they could focus on teaching in their classrooms. Helping one another is the norm. As one staff person explained, "No one says, 'that's not my job.' Further, everyone knows Mr. Martinez' expectation is that if there is a problem, you can come to him, but you also need to come with a solution."

Revere High School

Dr. Garcia, at Revere High School, was known quite similarly at his school. He created a school improvement council focused on "constructive ideas" and "workable solutions." The mission of the council was to provide an open forum for administrators, teachers, students, and parents to collaborate on ways Revere High School could better fulfill its mission. The council aims to ensure that the school continues to improve and continues to include all voices and members of the community in determining how to keep improving. Two students reflected on their experiences, by saying "It's a place kids can go if they have complaints or comments about the school; it gives you a voice. They teach you how to take action and make changes, rather than just complain." And, "Joining this team, I have more involvement. I feel more connected to the teachers and the principal."

When Dr. Garcia arrived at Revere High School seven years ago, the school was well on its way to a vision of student excellence. The continuity of district leadership allowed Revere's administration and faculty to remain focused on their efforts to increase rigor. Over the years, Revere had transitioned to college-ready graduation requirements and removed "watered down" courses from the curriculum that helped students earn credits, but not achieve success in college and life. This transition required extensive professional development to help teachers acquire the knowledge and skills to teach these more rigorous courses and to adopt higher academic expectations for their students. As a school community, Revere was committed to rigor, relationships, relevance and resilience and was making headway in those areas. Yet, due to multiple waves of immigration, more than 60 percent of Revere students did not speak English at home. Those changes were significant in how school personnel needed to support students. Administrators, faculty, and staff recognized the need to deepen their student-centered culture and personalize learning more for their students to help them achieve the 4Rs. Dr. Garcia began a multi-year process to improve instruction (discussed in Chapter Four), create a culture of collaboration, and build faculty and student connections. Although Revere had a foundation to build from, the shift to reach the next level required significant investment, communication and collaboration much like Mr. Martinez experienced and did at Eastlake.

The O'Farrell High School

Similar to Eastlake, O'Farrell started with a blank slate and a single ninth grade class. The initial ninth grade class at O'Farrell, however, included around 100–125 students, while Eastlake's initial class included around 500. Nonetheless, Mr. Rainey and the O'Farrell staff had the same goal: to be student-centered and focused on providing opportunities to students they would not otherwise have. Their commitment to staying student focused was one reason the school chose to remain relatively small, despite the demand. As one O'Farrell educator explained, ". . . the bigger the school, the more anonymity it creates for students. And, you have to work even harder at making every kid known."

The O'Farrell Charter School began as a middle school in 1994, transitioning to K-12 over twenty years. Mr. Rainey and his staff were very conscious of maintaining the culture of excellence as they grew and ensuring "that every kid gets what they need to be able to go to a four-year college, if that is what they want." To ensure the focus on each and every student, the school personnel took their time, running a ninth grade program for a couple of years and assessing their success before committing to becoming a full high school. And, those first couple of years, their scores on state tests were higher than most other San Diego Unified public schools, including those in the most affluent parts of the community. This convinced the O'Farrell team that they had to follow through and become a complete high school. In this transition, Mr. Rainey's strategy was to focus on being clear about who they were and who they weren't. "Ok, we're not that, we're this. But look at all the things we can do." He continued to explain how it was hard to convince students and parents to stay:

> They wanted to have football games. I didn't have football, I didn't have a separate campus. But, I had teachers who loved students. I said, "We will get your kids ready for college, and they will get the very best education."

The O'Farrell team took advantage of their size and built school spirit and engagement through fun activities like an air band competition and a turkey trot where everyone dressed up like Thanksgiving food. Also, if a problem arose, they had the flexibility to stop everything and bring all the kids out on the grass and discuss the issue. O'Farrell is structured around relationships, high standards and character development. They are a little bit like a small town community, according to Mr. Rainey. Their goal is to make sure no student falls through the cracks and if they fall, there is someone there to pick them up. They know their students have real trauma and challenges, as well as regular adolescent drama, and they want to be sure there is someone watching to make sure students are not derailed and can't find the path back to success.

Pace Early College High School

Things at Pace were a bit different for Principal Longoria when she arrived. It was a long-standing, low-performing school with a bad reputation in the community. As one student said, "People say it is a ghetto school." The facility was older and could not compete with other newer schools and extensive facilities for students to explore different opportunities. Parents didn't want their students to go to Pace and enrollment had been declining for years. As a result, they were unable to run some programs and it was hard to field an effective team or full, competitive band. This principal knew she needed to change long held beliefs about Pace and was determined to bring kids and families back. She would say, "Give me a chance. It is what we do in the school, not what the school looks like." Personally, she went out and recruited at the middle schools and was the school's first and biggest cheerleader.

Ms. Longoria's vision was to have the school recognized for the academic success of their students. When she arrived, she described Pace as a campus, "with a lot of need," but she saw the potential. Rather than viewing the students as deficient, she saw untapped potential. Moreover, she believed that it was even more important for her students who might have socio-economic and educational disadvantages to have access to the very best educational opportunities. Her view was that it was all the more necessary to provide exemplary educational experiences for Pace students, so that they could succeed in the outside world. She viewed it as her duty to make sure they were academically prepared to confront challenges she knew they would face and serve the community. When asked what she wanted us to remember about her school, she said,

> Every morning I say it—we educate students. That's what we do here, and we graduate leaders, and then we teach them to come back and serve here in the community. We empower our community. So, I would like for you to remember that, that all our kids here are educated. When they graduate, they're ready to be leaders, and then, they come back and they empower the community.

Yet, the students are not waiting until after graduation to serve the community. For the past three years, they have run, 'the big event'—a community service project. Last year, nearly 700 students participated. This year, they are going to plant trees around the community and are hoping for more participation. The students described, "That is our goal because there is nothing that Pace likes to do more than push us to be better and not just among ourselves, among our community as well." As a result of student activism in the community, students are beginning to be recognized by individuals throughout the city. Some of the students were going to present to the city council on what they were doing and also on ideas they had for improvements that the city could act on.

In addition to seeing potential in the students, Ms. Longoria saw potential and passion in the teachers. She knew that her teachers liked teaching and wanted to make a difference, but her biggest challenge was helping staff believe that they were going to be successful and that transformation was possible. To capitalize on this passion and to change mindsets, she spoke candidly with the staff about the need to change what they were doing. She called them honest or courageous conversations and would say, "We have to choose—we can't keep teaching the way we have. I know you are passionate about what you do, but we have to change to meet the needs of our kids now." Her approach was based on the basic principle she described as "help me help you." She did not want staff to feel alone or unsure about what to do and she made sure to have an open door, so staff could come to her and her team to ask for help. Her clear priority that she communicated was teaching comes first and we all must do whatever is necessary to remove barriers to ensure high quality teaching and learning. And, they started there and rolled up their sleeves and began working together, trying to do their best every day. Everyone in the building, no matter their role, knew they must support teaching and what occurred in the classrooms.

Now, Principal Longoria describes Pace as, "powerful, innovative, college ready and fun." They are a team that supports one another and does whatever is needed to get the job done. Each member holds a piece of the puzzle and Mrs. Longoria provides the vision and keeps the team focused on what is important. Her leadership team understands the charge and tries to stay true to the principles she models and espouses. Her Dean of Instruction said her interactions with teachers start with, "What can we do to make it better? How can we help you? Help us help you. That's what we've learned from her. That's the school of thought that we follow. It is all about helping and serving."

Essential Elements of a School Vision

Student success, based on high standards, guided all of these leaders. Each of the principals believed in their students and felt their role as educators was to support students to meet the expectations they set. They

Figure 2.1 Essential Elements of a School Vision

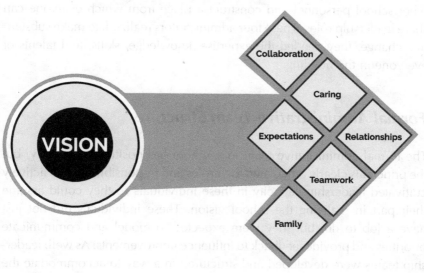

experienced different opportunities and challenges and their school mottos sound different, but relationships, caring, collaboration, expectations, teamwork, and family were unifying principles described by stakeholders at all four schools (see Figure 2.1).

Distributed Leadership: Team Structure and Beyond

Leading a school toward its vision of excellence and equity is challenging, at best. Principals, in addition to setting the vision and establishing a climate and culture that both allows and requires high-quality work, by staff and students, must organize who does what and how the team works and communicates with one another. Recent scholarship contends that building a team is essential to developing and sustaining a high-performing urban school (Spillane, 2006; Wallace, 2013). We observed that all four principals created a shared or distributed leadership structure across their campuses. By this, we mean leadership was distributed to those capable and willing to develop knowledge and expertise to support the school goals. This included both the traditional administrative or leadership team as well as anyone else willing to step up and assume leadership for school priorities. Ideas are welcomed, and staff are treated as professionals. Administrators intentionally seek to develop the ideas of teachers and other school personnel and construct a place from which everyone can share leadership roles. These four administrators realized, to make substantive change, they needed the expertise, knowledge, skills, and talents of everyone in the building.

Formal Administrative Team Structure

The formal administrative team in a school has positional authority, but the principals clearly articulated their roles and responsibilities and actively cultivated leadership capacity in these individuals so they could assume their part in realizing the school vision. These individuals did not just have a job to do, but they were expected to model and communicate priorities and provide feedback to influence improvements. As well, leadership teams were developed and structured in a way to accommodate the strengths of individuals and manage transitions that naturally occur. For example, at Pace, one of the assistant principals, who had been there six years was leaving to assume the principalship of another school in the district. Rather than being concerned about what would happen with his departure, Rose Longoria knew the team would fill in the gaps and support whomever took the position. It may have meant a redistribution of responsibilities to accommodate each individual's strengths and weaknesses, but she and her team were confident the leadership change would not affect school operations and student outcomes. Similarly, Pace and Eastlake each had two new assistant principals in the school year we visited. Team members reflected that the changes required adjustments to sustain interactions where each team member knew, almost instinctively, what the other was doing, but there was clarity in the roles and responsibilities so the daily work of the school would still be accomplished.

In some cases, the principals hired new administrators and sought particular skills and in others they were assigned to the school. As Ms. Longoria said, "We just take them under our wing, and they're part of our family now . . . We work side by side. It's not us and them. No. It's all of us."

The three large, comprehensive high schools had similar administrative team structures with slight variations. What was common across all three was that each element of the school program was monitored to make sure it was contributing to important goals.

Revere High School

Revere had a deputy principal who helped manage operations and four assistant principals, each of whom had responsibility for one grade level. In their role, they described that they were, "primarily focused on student progress towards graduation, discipline, and classroom management needs on a daily basis." These folks were the day-to-day, operational building team. As a group, they met informally weekly and formally every other week. As they explained, "We work as a team as much as possible because in the role, there is no way we could be successful if we don't balance one another and work together." They are supported by a staff of five directors who work across the district with primary responsibility for ensuring that curriculum is aligned, teachers are supported, and instructional coaches have the strategies to work with teachers.

Pace Early College High School

Pace has a similar structure; however, rather than a deputy, there is a dean of instruction and four assistant principals who each have a grade level responsibility and department-level responsibility. The principal and dean of instruction have primary responsibility for instruction and the teachers and each of the APs has one major work area, like the Early College High School program or the data-management system. Pace was fortunate to have a core team of three members who had been at the school over five years. Over the years, they had cross-trained and learned different sets of responsibilities that contributed to their growth and expertise. The roles they assumed currently reflected their strengths and the needs of the school. Mrs. Longoria was committed to growing her leadership team but made decisions about who would do what based on school needs and ensuring nothing would falter. For example, one of the assistant principals was assigned the master schedule and data management system. The master schedule required tweaking to better serve the Pace students and she knew she needed someone with patience and focus to work through the details and be responsive to individual student needs. The leadership team, though, often shares responsibilities and backs one another up to make sure everything gets done and no one feels alone or like they are working more than anyone else. As the dean of instruction said, "We're like the Marines; we leave no man behind." This provides a level of safety and security as expertise is shared and grown in others. This is not to say that tasks always occur smoothly. The leaders have strong opinions. They will "fight it out and then have to get over their own egos" if a decision made by Mrs. Longoria doesn't go their way. Given the clarity in purpose at Pace, they know, without a doubt, when a decision is made, it is in "students' best interests."

Eastlake High School

Similarly, Eastlake has five assistant principals who each oversee select departments and grade levels. Annually, they review the data from the prior year, set goals, and work with department chairs to translate goals to specific tasks and objectives to be pursued with various teachers. Although Eastlake is a distinguished school with student performance exceeding state averages, they always focus on ways to improve. This year, staff noted they did not receive the highest distinction in English and worked as a team to determine how everyone could support development of these necessary skills for students. As a result, their first campus-wide professional development was focused on writing across the curriculum. All departments learned ways to support writing in their disciplines, as they realized students needed more practice, attention, and feedback.

Assistant principals met with grade level teams on Mondays, with department chairs on Tuesdays, and with department teams on Fridays to make sure communication was clear, reached everyone, and everyone had the opportunity to participate in decision-making. The formal leadership team also includes two secondary intervention coaches that are essentially deans of curriculum according to Mr. Martinez. He explained, "They make sure the curriculum is being followed. They make sure AP and dual credit are up to par, and they make sure the ESL kids are being served appropriately."

The O'Farrell High School

Each of the larger high schools had a compliment of assistant principals as well as staff identified as department chairs and other staff who were instructional coaches to support the school to reach their instructional and learning goals for students. O'Farrell, due to its size, has a different structure, but nonetheless is committed to the same goals and principles of collaboration, respect and inclusion. The formal structure at O'Farrell includes a superintendent who oversees the elementary, middle, high school, and independent study school each of which has its own principal. As the school grew, Dr. Dean, the superintendent made a conscious effort to not add administrative staff. He wanted their resources utilized on instruction at the classroom level, to be able to fully meet the needs of all their students. The high school does have department chairs that Mr. Rainey relies on to lead the content teams. He said, he realized early on that he needed to delegate and trust people if they were going to provide the opportunities students needed and accomplish their goals of all students matriculating into postsecondary options upon graduation. The school hired an academic coach in the last few years who works across the three schools. She oversees the English learner program and coaches team and department leaders who then coach and support their teams. Mr. Rainey also has one team leader at the high school, who gets an extra prep period to help him with administrative matters. But, generally, teachers step up to the plate and run various programs and activities. On the day we visited, O'Farrell had "Signing Day." It was a school-wide event to celebrate the colleges all seniors had chosen to attend the following fall. Mr. Rainey entrusted staff to plan and run the event. He explained:

> I treat people like professionals. I trust them. When they mess up, everybody does, a nudge is all people need to get back on track. And, it usually doesn't happen again. If it happens again, then we have a talk.

Teacher Leadership

In addition to the formal administrative structure in place, each of the schools also offered and created multiple opportunities for teacher leadership. At Revere High School, Dr. Garcia, the principal said, "This school right now is led by teachers to be honest with you, entirely by teachers." By this, he was referring to their leadership with professional development and 12 different student-centered learning committees that were thinking through the school's next phase of development across all the departments (e.g., literacy), programs (e.g., advisory), and initiatives (e.g., the academic portfolio or device media). The School Redesign and Innovation Team (SRIT)—a group of teachers and administrators- oversees the work. Teachers choose the committee they are interested in; it does not have to be related to their department. For example, the literacy committee is made up of staff from the English, math, science, history, and art departments. Of course, Dr. Garcia has a vision and oversees the work of the campus, but this system captures the expertise and passions of everyone in the building to improve on and grow the initiatives and direction. These committees provide feedback and sometimes they push back when they disagree with the overall direction. However, together they move forward with buy-in at all levels of the organization.

Mr. Martinez operationalized the idea of teacher leadership in a different way but was intentional about wanting to unleash the power of teachers to contribute to the change and improvement at Eastlake. Teachers were considered and called instructional leaders. Some took on additional responsibilities as department chairs and grade level specialists to create additional teacher leadership opportunities. Mr. Martinez was purposeful in creating a clear structure across all staff in the building as he wanted to ensure and allow information to filter through the system in many ways. His goal was "to not slow them [the staff] down. They know what they want to do. And you have to create that structure to support everyone and improvement."

Professionalism and Respect

At all four schools, we found that all staff members were treated with respect. There was an acknowledgement that each staff person owned a particular expertise. There was recognition that no one person could be expert in all the diverse aspects of running a high school. Everyone was needed to help make all students college and career ready.

To that end, all four principals intentionally trained their leadership team so they could assume important responsibilities in ways that reflected a sincere respect for all staff members. Ms. Longoria was known to bring her team into what she called courageous conversations so they could observe and learn. She knew this was often the most difficult aspect of leadership, giving difficult feedback and/or confronting beliefs that did not align with the schools' vision. "My job as a leader is to train them so they can become leaders." Members of the leadership teams across schools noted that their principal not only communicated decisions; they took the time to explain why the decision was made.

As well, principals had to make sure staff were not over-committing themselves. Staff were so willing to assume leadership roles that principals had to work to ensure that teachers focused their energy and commitment primarily on students in their classrooms and improving instruction. Administrators at all schools described their job as making sure teachers could be successful. And, principals believed their job was to train administrators, so they could become leaders. Leaders were adamant about makings decisions that were in the best interest of students, not staff, but leaders also fully understood and knew that they were responsible for ensuring staff felt valued, supported and respected. The leaders believed that teachers were most likely to feel valued, supported and respected when they were effective in their roles, so supporting teachers was ultimately in the best interest of students.

Transparency in Expectations and Communication

These complex school communities would not function without the clear, consistent communication of expectations for both students and staff. One concrete way all the schools accomplished this was by having principals and administrators who were both visible and approachable. Approach-ability ensured issues were raised and did not fester in ways that damaged the culture. Staff could express concerns and ask for what they needed. Administrators described trying to put aside their tasks and give folks their undivided attention. Although the administrators expressed the importance of sometimes saying "no," or having "courageous meetings" when things were not working or teachers were not improving, they primarily wanted to provide support and that meant doing the little things that truly told teachers they were heard. For example, a teacher at Revere described having difficulty with students following a new policy she implemented in her room that phones needed to be put in docking stations in a certain area in the room. She felt the phones were distracting students; but, students were resisting the new procedure. She talked with her assistant principal about her frustration. The AP came by the next day and just stood near the docking station as students came into the room. To the teacher, it felt like she had an ally and helped smooth the situation for students.

Visibility

Visibility in classrooms, hallways, meetings, and events allowed for opportunities for praise and feedback to reinforce critical priorities related to the school culture, curriculum, or instruction. For example, frequent walkthroughs are conducted to emphasize school-wide areas of emphasis, such as using higher-order thinking questions with students. Administrators and other leaders used praise abundantly to recognize small changes and acknowledge staff efforts to do things differently than they had before. Often praise took small forms, such as a "thumbs up" as the observer left the classroom door or a follow-up text message with a specific comment about something observed. At Revere, teachers talked about the constant communication with administration and noted that when administrators walked through their classrooms, they always provided feedback. One teacher described it this way:

> [The administrators' feedback] is always very supportive in the sense that it's always pointing out something that you're doing really well. And then, there is always a question to push you one step further. So, even if you have all of those backbone pieces in place, it's like, "Have you thought of this?" They are there to support you and push you to be better educators. They are not against you.

Changing commitments, expectations and mindsets takes time and support. By being visible, school leaders created multiple opportunities to:

1. assess how teachers and other school personnel felt,
2. determine how they could address teachers' needs, and
3. talk about priorities.

In addition, the heightened visibility of administrators allowed others to observe them as role models, as they interacted with students, parents, and other school personnel. These leaders knew they needed to articulate clearly what was important and why. But, they also knew that they needed to demonstrate through their own actions what was important and why.

Students quite frequently commented on the visibility of school leaders. Students perceived that their school administrators were interested in their success and committed to them and their fellow students. For example, a student at Pace said, "The administrators support us. They walk into our room and they ask, 'How are you guys?' They always pump us up. We have the support from administration and our teachers. They are all so dedicated." Similarly, a student at Eastlake reflected:

> We all support each other. Students support students, teachers support students, and our principals support everyone. Our assistant principals are always at games and are always in the classroom making sure we are learning. They want to see

we are really working, and I think that's really good support, like knowing that they care about us.

Clearly Defined Roles

Expectations and roles are clearly defined so that there is little confusion and each stakeholder, in his or her role, can make decisions when needed. There are few bottlenecks and teachers waste little time waiting for answers. There is a role for everyone and everyone has a job to do. Leaders at these school sites recognized they were ultimately responsible for what happened at their school, but they did not have to be involved in every decision. They empowered staff to make decisions and since expectations and priorities were clear, they were confident all the daily decisions that needed to get made each day would reflect the school values. They embodied a "come with me" type of attitude and style (Goleman, 2000). Leaders provided the vision and stated the end goal, but gave staff the leeway to determine the path, innovate and devise solutions. Principals were in charge of the school, but they also conveyed that everyone had a role and explained how each person's role contributed to the larger vision and mission for the school.

Staff believed what they did mattered and they knew why their work mattered. By repeatedly talking about what was important, modeling what was important and rewarding those who made efforts to pursue what mattered, the principals were able to create an environment in which priorities were obvious and progress was continuous. Feedback, both positive and constructive, reminded staff about key issues. For example, at all four schools, respecting students is a high priority. Principals modeled this and frequently discussed how everyone was an equal member of the community. Principals and other administrators confronted staff if they observed behavior that was not respectful of students. Being direct and straightforward with all stakeholders was a common theme.

Of course, administrators disciplined students as needed; however, they administered consequences fairly and in a manner that respected each student and allowed the student to retain a sense of dignity. Consequences were designed to promote reflection and better choices more than they were designed to punish students. For example, if a student was not getting to school on time, rather than suspend, a staff member would pick the student up and drive him or her to school. The student clearly understood that the goal was their regular attendance and school success.

Clarity about expectations and roles led students to know that what they did mattered and why it mattered. Students often did an excellent job of conveying to their peers what was important and why. For example, O'Farrell has a very clear uniform policy. Kids, across the country, daily try to push limits in regard to uniforms. A new student to O'Farrell was no different. When a staff member pointed out issues about the student's attire, the student had a ready excuse. So, the student's peers stepped in and explained the uniform policy and why it was important to follow it. They described they were respected, but they needed to do their part and follow the rules.

One Pace administrator shared, "Ms. Longoria is humble, but clearly the one in charge although she shares everything, . . . to help folks take ownership." At Revere High School, Principal Garcia, commented that "leadership is based on collaboration and shared decision making," because

Figure 2.2 Shared Leadership Practices

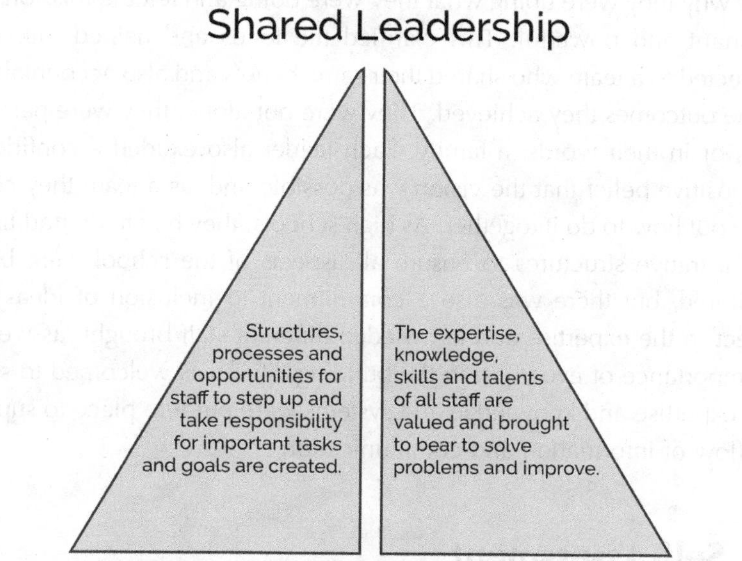

Shared Leadership

Structures, processes and opportunities for staff to step up and take responsibility for important tasks and goals are created.

The expertise, knowledge, skills and talents of all staff are valued and brought to bear to solve problems and improve.

Transparency in expectations and clear communication are the foundation.

he felt it leads to ownership on the part of the teachers, staff, students, and parents. Clear expectations and clear communication about expectations contributed to everyone (teachers, support staff, administrators, students, and parents) feeling ownership and a sense of belonging.

Conclusion

Meaningful school improvement requires change and collective, focused effort. Often, we find school staffs are working hard, but not making progress or achieving their goals, which can be dispiriting. They become tired, frustrated, and, at worst, angry. This often causes people to blame students or look outside the school walls for reasons for their lack of success. If they are working hard, it must be something else and consequently there is not much they can do. Leaders in these schools nurtured a powerful sense of purpose for their work while simultaneously clarifying everyone's roles and responsibilities in that process. The reason for the work provided motivation and meaning in all of these high schools. They knew why they were doing what they were doing and felt the mission was important and powerful. This clarified the focus and helped folks feel connected to a team who shared their same beliefs and also accountability for the outcomes they achieved. They were not alone; they were part of a team, or in their words, a family. Each leader also exuded a confidence and positive belief that the vision was possible and, as a team they could figure out how to do it together. As high schools, they had fairly traditional administrative structures to ensure all aspects of the school were being monitored, but there was also a commitment to inclusion of ideas and respect in the expertise and knowledge different staff brought, as well as the importance of every job in the building. Staff was welcomed to share their expertise and knowledge and systems were put into place to support that flow of information and communication.

Self-Assessment

1) Can all school stakeholders articulate the school vision and explain what it means?

a) Is the vision based on rigorous expectations for all students? Are there groups of students for whom the vision does not seem to apply? What evidence suggests that teachers and students are being held to high standards?

b) Are there concrete, measurable goals for student performance (academic, behavioral, interpersonal)? How are they perceived by staff?

c) Are the core strategies to reach the school goals articulated?

2) How would you describe your school's brand?

a) What attributes or descriptors do you hope students will think of first when they hear your school name?

b) Does the brand reflect a commitment to each student's growth and success?

c) How do you hope alumni will describe their experiences?

3) How do you and your leadership staff communicate your expectations to both students and teachers?

4) How have you distributed roles and responsibilities across your leadership team?

a) What happens to help ensure that leadership team members are assuming those responsibilities effectively?

b) In what ways are leadership team members responsible for modeling and supporting important elements of the school culture?

5) What opportunities are there for staff to step up and take leadership for important school priorities?

a) What happens to help ensure that school personnel are supported so they can assume those responsibilities effectively?

b) What happens to help ensure that school personnel are not overwhelmed by assuming too many responsibilities?

6) Which rules, procedures, and routines feel like a tug-a-war between administrators and teachers or between teachers and students? Conversely, which rules, procedures, and routines are "owned" by everyone, such that everyone shares responsibility?

References

Chenoweth, K., & Theokas, C. (2012). The professional educator: Leading for Learning. *American Educator, 36*(3), 24.

Goleman, D. (2000). Leadership that gets results. *Harvard Business Review.* March–April, pp. 316. Boston, MA: Harvard Business School Publishing.

Johnson, J. F., Uline, C. L., & Perez, L. G. (2017). *Leadership in America's best urban schools.* New York: Routledge.

Leithwood, K., Louis, K. S., Anderson, S., & Wahlstrom, K. (2004). *Review of research: How leadership influences student learning.* Retrieved from Wallace Foundation website: www.wallacefoundation.org/knowledge-center/school-leadership/key-research/documents/how-leadership-influences-student-learning.pdf

Louis, K. S., Leithwood, K., Wahlstrom, K., & Anderson, S. (2010). *Investigating the links to improved student learning: Final report of research findings.* Retrieved from Wallace Foundation website: www.wallacefoundation.org/knowledge-center/schoolleadership/key-research/Documents/Investigating-the-Links-to-Improved-Student-Learning.pdf

Marzano, R. J., Waters, T., & McNulty, B. A. (2005). *School leadership that works: From research to results.* Alexandria, VA: ASCD.

Spillane, J. P. (2006). *Distributed leadership.* San Francisco, CA: Jossey-Bass.

Waters, J. T., Marzano, R. J., & McNulty, B. A. (2003). *Balanced leadership: What 30 years of research tells us about the effect of leadership on student achievement.* Aurora, CO: Mid-continent Research for Education and Learning.

Wallace Foundation, The. (2013). *The school principal as leader: Guiding schools to better teaching and learning.* New York: The Wallace Foundation.

3 | **Fostering Student-Centered Values**

> *I think our kids feel a part of something. They know that they're missed when they're not here. We just really care about our kids, like a lot. We notice when they're not here. We get when they're having a bad day. And as Chantal was saying, we love on them. I don't have kids, but I would imagine it's how a parent feels. Like, you want what's best for them but you care deeply when they're having a bad day, you figure out how to balance both. And I would hope our kids feel that.*
>
> *—O'Farrell Teacher*

In the four urban high schools we studied, educators strived to make Latino students and their families feel valued, respected, and capable. They provided a welcoming, caring, clean, and safe school environment. They helped Latino parents perceive that their children had futures full of promise and showed parents how they could support their children toward that promise. As well, school personnel promoted a learning environment that empowered Latino students to feel academically capable, while reinforcing students' linguistic, cultural, artistic, and athletic strengths and talents.

Such an optimistic approach to the education of Latino students stands in contrast to the history of Latino students in the public education system. Often, school system policies and procedures treated Latino students and their families as if they had deficits that required instruction that was remedial and segregated. Recent studies still find that Latino students are seen as "disadvantaged" by their language and culture (Garcia & Guera, 2004; Rolon, 2005). For example, one study found that Latino English learners received an inferior education along seven different dimensions, even when compared to other poor and low-income students (Gándara, et al., 2003). Chief among the educational inequities suffered were teachers unprepared to address students' needs. In contrast, the teachers in our study schools acknowledged, appreciated, and integrated Latino students' identities into school life and curriculum and simultaneously maintained high and rigorous standards that would prepare their students for college. This was done in both the schools with an all Latino population and many Latino educators, as well as in the schools with heterogeneous student populations. One teacher described why they thought they were successful with Latino students:

> We have kids who have been here a short amount of time and are already speaking English, writing it, reading it and doing a lot better than you'd think. I think a big part of it is that they feel understood. They feel there's an awareness of what they're coming with, what tools they have, what skills they have and how we can help them move forward.

At another school, a teacher explained it this way:

> I am intentional in class, pairing up students who are struggling with a concept with a peer I know they are going to be able to speak Spanish with to help explain and under- stand things. It's not validating. It's valuing. We embrace our students' culture and their language. And, we think about how we can bring that to the forefront of what we're doing.

Bazron, Osher, and Fleischman (2005) provided the following four recommendations to better serve students from culturally and linguistically diverse backgrounds:

1. Set high expectations and provide a "scaffold of support" rather than tracking students into low-level classes;
2. Give students direct instruction in the "hidden curriculum" of the school (which courses to take, which teachers to seek out, test importance, how to study, etc.);

3. Create environments that allow students and teachers to connect with one another, both in and out of the classroom; and

4. Use the cultural knowledge, prior experience, and frames of reference of students in classroom instruction to strengthen student connectedness to school.

In the exemplary schools we studied, educators attempted to create an additive, rather than a subtractive, schooling experience for their Latino students as described in the recommendations above. Administrators, teachers, and staff approached Latino students' education from a shared set of core values that guided their actions (see Figure 3.1). In these schools, educators believed that Latino students had promising futures and that their families were critical partners in achieving the promise. Educators believed that a welcoming, safe and caring school environment was central to student success. Finally, the educators in these schools believed that their Latino students' linguistic and cultural backgrounds were assets to be leveraged. Consequently, teachers built upon their students' life experiences and funds of knowledge to provide deep, rich and intellectually challenging instruction that pushed students to excel.

Figure 3.1 Core Student Centered Values

APPRECIATION OF LINGUISTIC AND CULTURAL ASSETS

WELCOMING, SAFE AND CARING ENVIRONMENT

FUTURES FULL OF PROMISE

FAMILIES AS PARTNERS

STUDENT CENTERED VALUES

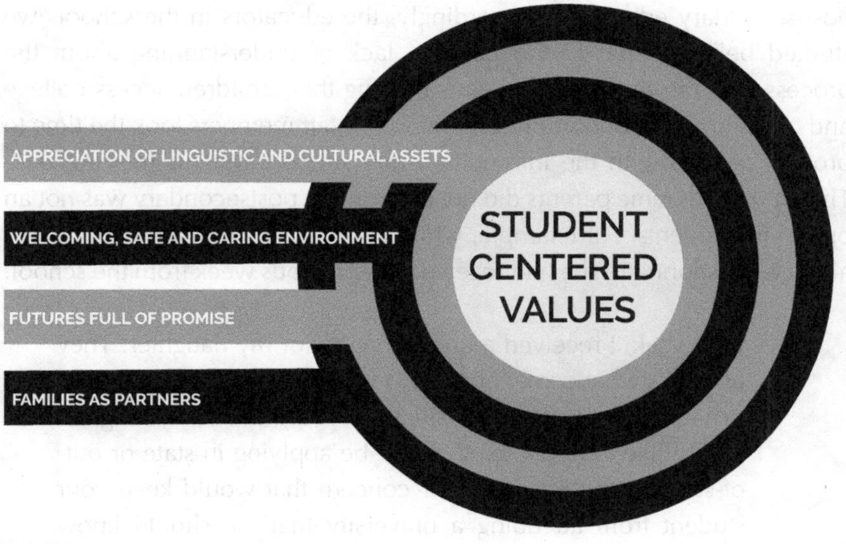

Families as Partners

Across the schools we studied, administrators believed strongly in the need for partnerships with their students' families. They understood that they could not achieve their goal of student readiness for postsecondary options without the support of family members. Students are seen as active participants in the educational process and need to be engaged and interested and families are the first teachers of their children and can encourage and support them to take on new challenges at school. As such, school personnel ensured parents had information about school goals, expectations and opportunities, and felt welcome in the school. As a result, parents and guardians felt valued as equal members of the team. They were then better able to communicate their children's goals, concerns, strengths and needs, related to English language development, acceleration, or access to programs such as music, engineering, or sports. As a Pace Early College High School parent explained, "There have been times when I come to open house, I come to activities, and administration is always telling us 'tell us what you need.' We are given that comfort to come, at any time, to them."

In these very successful schools, as in other schools that serve large populations of Latino students, many of the parents were educated outside of the United States and never had the opportunity to go to college, leaving them unaware of the steps necessary to negotiate the complicated path to post-secondary education. Accordingly, the educators in the schools we studied believed that Latino parents' lack of understanding about the process stood in the way of parents helping their children access college and career training opportunities; therefore, staff members took the time to provide parents with the information and support systems they needed. They did not assume parents did not care or that postsecondary was not an option for students. For example, while visiting O'Farrell, a parent told us about a questionnaire she had received the previous week from the school.

> Last week, I received a questionnaire for my daughter. They asked us what career choice do you want for your daughter? What university or universities do you think your daughter would like to apply to? Will she be applying in-state or out-of-state? Is there an issue or concern that would keep your student from attending a university that we should know

about? I like the questionnaire because they care about our students and us. The resources each family has may be different. My daughter wants to go to New York to study, so then they let me know these are the resources she can tap into.

Communication Strategies

Given this commitment to families, each of the schools invested time and effort into communicating effectively with them. At these high schools, communication with families is conducted in various ways to provide multiple opportunities and create an open door feel. As in most schools, the administrators and teachers communicate face-to-face with families via events, such as parent-teacher conferences, open houses, and regular parent-teacher organization meetings. As well, the schools hold pep rallies and invite the community to special events. Yet, recognizing that some parents might be unable to attend these and other in-person events, the educators in these very successful high schools also rely on phone calls, email, and social media for more consistent communication with families. The parent of a Revere High School student explained her approach to communicating with the school:

> I usually email them, and they are pretty good about getting back to me within a day. I mean, they look at the message. If they see it is urgent, I'm going to get a message back right away. And if not, I'll get a message by the next day.

As a teacher at Eastlake explained, communicating with parents opens the door to building relationships with students:

> I have emails with parents almost day to day, depending on the students. It helps being in touch with [parents] because you are able to find out about the kid and more about their family and everything they are going through. I teach Bio-Med and most kids go through stuff or have a family member that has gone through stuff and it helps to be able to talk about it. And then you just build a relationship from there.

And when communication fails, educators at these very successful urban high schools have strategies in place to close the gap. They assume parents want to be involved so they find ways to promote communication and, unlike staff at some schools, they don't sabotage their efforts by assuming that parents will not reciprocate. Educators in these four schools recognized that all parents are not on the same schedules and might not be available for meetings at customary times. Instead, educators assumed responsibility for reaching out and ensuring that parents could participate. An Eastlake teacher described her efforts to make sure she met with every parent of the students in the ESL program:

> At the beginning of each year, I meet the parents in my program. This was the [initial meeting] date. Well, five of my students and parents couldn't make it. So then, I set up several additional meetings, as I tried to reach all the parents. Then, some still couldn't make it. So, I called the individual parents to see what was convenient. I asked, "When is it good for you to come in?"

Barriers to communication are a real challenge that all schools faced. Many parents in these schools struggle to support their families and work more than one job, or are too intimidated to come to school due to language barriers, so educators work to remove those barriers. In fact, most of the schools actively worked to make sure they had numerous staff who could communicate effectively with parents. Administrators ensured that front office staff included those who were fluent in their families' languages. When necessary, teachers enlisted the help of Spanish-speaking colleagues when communicating with families in person or on the phone. The English language paraprofessional at O'Farrell commented that she often translated at IEP meetings. She reflected that although it was difficult to translate the academic language for parents and remain objective during emotional meetings, she was eager to do it, as she was a familiar face for parents and was able to put them at ease.

Additional Resources

Both Pace and Eastlake also had part-time parent liaisons who helped bridge the gap with families and further support communication and connection to the school. The parent liaison at Eastlake told us she was in the process of contacting parents to let them know teachers had referred their children for tutoring. In this case, all the parents she was contacting had students who were earning good grades, but their teachers noticed they had struggled on the recent benchmark assessment. End-of-course tests were coming up that students needed to pass for graduation and the teachers wanted to give their students a little extra help. However, they wanted parents' permission as students were going to be pulled from the last five minutes of class and would miss the first hour of sports practice one or two days a week. She went on to further explain these conversations were really important as it gave the school the opportunity to talk with parents about priorities and validate school goals.

In addition to supporting home-school communication, these staff members also provided trainings and opportunities for parents to grow their language and advocacy skills. The parent liaison at Eastlake was very proud of a mother-daughter conference they hosted on a Saturday for 1,200 participants. The liaisons strive to do things that support families and create a strong community with shared values. Both schools are also fortunate to partner with Communities in Schools (CIS) to help their low-income, struggling students and families access resources to thwart drop out issues and keep students on the path to graduation. One CIS school-based coordinator said, "We really, really, really focus on the family and make sure students are ok at home, so they can focus here at school."

Not all of the schools had additional resources to meet the needs of their families, but they still tried to connect with families and build relationships. For example, Revere High School runs a Parent Leadership Training Institute to empower parents to be change agents in their students' lives and in the community. Also, in the interest of encouraging more immigrant parents to socialize with the English-speaking parents, Revere hosted a set of home economic activities for parents and their children in the Learning Commons. One parent who participated shared that these activities provided her with a window into what was going on in school as the Learning Commons overlooked other active school areas.

Frequent Interactions

Each of these four exemplary schools made frequent calls home to reinforce their connection and build trust with parents. One teacher explained:

We call all the time. We are encouraged to call anytime a student is failing, anytime a student is doing bad, but also when a student is doing well. So those [calling when the student is doing well] are my favorite phone calls because the parents are just like, 'What did he do now?' And I get to say, 'He helped someone.' So, those are fun to do. But it is important. I think this in particular, because we have a wide range of students. We have students who are experiencing poverty and growing up with little. We also have students who are pretty wealthy in this area. It's important to be able to see the different types of students we have and understand their background. And the best way to do that is talking to parents, talking to students.

These actions are not rote, practiced interactions. Rather, they reflect the schools' underlying value that parents are partners in the process. Teachers in these schools believe that parents can provide invaluable information about their students. Teachers also believe that through their frequent interactions with parents, they not only learn more about their students' home environments, but they can also help parents learn more about school practices and activities. Recognizing and acknowledging parents over and over again as partners in helping students achieve their goals strengthens connections that both the schools and families valued.

Welcoming, Caring and Safe Environment

First and foremost, these schools are welcoming environments for all stakeholders. For Latino families, school personnel acknowledge and appreciate that the Latino community regards educators with respect, so they ensure that parents are treated with respect and kindness at all times. According to a Revere parent, "They make you feel welcome. They always have a smile on their face. They're always interested in what's going on in your life and telling you what's going on in the building." Similarly, when we spoke with parents at O'Farrell, a parent told us about the warm welcome parents received on the first day of school:

One thing that had a great impact on me was the first day of classes. Everyone was greeting us. Everyone gave me a nice welcome even if they didn't know me, everyone was saying "Good morning, how can we help you? Are you new, are you looking for a particular room?" That had a big impact on me, the way they treated you.

Another O'Farrell parent noted that the school leadership played a critical role in helping students and families feel welcome:

I hadn't seen a principal waiting outside to greet students and then here, at the high school level, Mr. Rainey is out there every day. They try to know students by their name as well as the parents, 'Good morning, Ms. Mendoza.' It is like a family, like a small family, comfortable and friendly.

During our visits to these schools, we noted that school staff members were out in the hallways during passing periods chatting with students or asking about the results of a recent game or event. Everyone on staff is part of the culture of welcoming students and families into the school environment. As one staff member put it, "Everybody is respectful. Everything comes, in my point of view, from administrators in how they treat the kids. And from the administration, it goes to the teachers, staff, everyone. And that's what kids see and that's why they're good."

A Real Family Atmosphere

Being welcoming is just the first step. In these schools, a culture of a home away from home has been created intentionally. Educators want students and staff, as well as families, to feel safe and comfortable. As one staff member explained:

I think the care here is a big thing. You can see it walking into the school, like the warmth of the family. It sounds corny, but it is true. I worked at another school. You just didn't feel it. Here, you feel it. You walk in the halls, [and] you feel the family.

In very successful urban schools, educators take concrete steps to demonstrate their caring. They believe strongly that once the kids know they are loved, they will work harder. We heard this multiple times, in multiple ways from all stakeholder groups, especially students. School personnel create a culture of caring through small actions, like knowing students by name, and by choosing programs for the school, based on student interests. One teacher described it this way:

> I think our kids feel a part of something. They know that they're missed when they're not here. . . . We just really care about our kids, like a lot. Like, we notice when they're not here. We get it when they're having a bad day. And as [my colleague] was saying, we love on them. I don't have kids, but I would imagine it's how a parent feels. Like, you want what's best for them but you care deeply when they're having a bad day, and you figure out to do both.

Building Relationships

In these four schools, it's all about relationships. School personnel understand that strong relationships between students and teachers provide the foundation for learning and that these relationships do not happen by accident—they are built through caring and trust. Figure 3.2 displays the key qualities of these student–teacher relationships. Consequently, each school has crafted its own unique system to foster strong teacher/student relationships. Each school established norms and expectations and created opportunities and experiences for staff and students to get to know one

Figure 3.2 Qualities of Student–Teacher Relationships

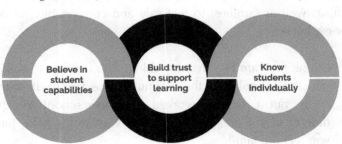

Believe in student capabilities

Build trust to support learning

Know students individually

another. For example, both Revere and O'Farrell have a short (advisory) period built into their schedule that is specifically designed to ensure that each student has at least one staff member who knows them well and can serve as a point of contact for the student and family. Students are assigned to the same mentor for their four years of high school. Both students and staff value the opportunity to form these very close and meaningful relationships. Students perceived the adults knew and cared about them and the adults got to know the students personally. Educators understood the barriers students faced associated with poverty, trauma, neighborhood violence, but also, educators understood their students' hopes and expectations. This helped the educators invest the energy to pursue instructional and curricula transformations that would help their students learn and achieve their goals.

When Rose Longoria got to Pace, it was evident that the school was facing many challenges and the pressure was on to change those outcomes. One of the greatest challenges was the loss of enrollment, which adversely impacted the academic, athletic and fine arts programs. Pace was the only high school in Brownsville that had not met the criteria for Adequate Yearly Progress (part of the accountability criteria under the No Child Left Behind Act). Pace was identified as a Priority school by the state, meaning that there was significant room for improvement. But when asked the first thing she did, she reflected it was all about relationships and changing the culture. Staff did not see the potential in their students and the students had also internalized this belief. Her first conversations with the staff were about the need to get to know the students. "We need to understand our students. We need to build relationships. Let's find out why they are struggling. What's going on?" She knew she needed to build systems and procedures to build teacher capacity and better support the learning needs of students, but she also realized this would not happen if they did not truly see their kids and believe in them. She wanted to build a team that was committed to the students and knew them individually. Now Mrs. Longoria described the culture this way, "Lots of love and a lot of care goes into what we do. Students come first . . . Students know it and when they see that there's a caring heart, it makes a lot of difference." Students feel comfortable approaching staff members, confiding in them or asking for help. One teacher explained that a paradigm shift occurred after this investment in knowing more about the students as individuals, "They believe they are better."

Empowering Students

Relationships, built on trust and caring, helped empower students to take on new challenges and opportunities and to persist even when it was difficult. When interviewing students at these four schools, we often heard comments similar to the one made by an Eastlake student who said, "Probably something I like most about the teachers here is that they're always there to help." The students expressed their appreciation in having teachers and other school personnel who were "on their side." This helped create a safety net so nothing was beyond reach, including things students never thought they would do. One student shared, "They always give you great advice and always push you to go further, so you reach your potential basically." Another student described how he was struggling in calculus and feeling like he wanted to drop the class. The teacher convinced him to stick with it and by second semester, he was doing pretty well. But, as he explained, the challenges persisted, but so did his teacher:

> It started again to get really, really stressful for me and I was like, no more calculus. I don't care. And then she told me, "I think you really can pass the Advanced Placement test. I truly think that you can get a 5." I was like, "Ms. Margo I don't know if I can get a 5, maybe like a 4 or 3 or maybe a 2.0, if I really try." They really push you and they encourage you in ways that make you think you can do one more thing, but they think you can do ten times more.

These are caring educators, but they also demand that students work hard and succeed in what they do. Knowing the students, trust and consistency are necessary to be able to demand excellent work. Many schools fall into the trap of taking care of and nurturing their students, but this is insufficient to accomplish rigorous learning goals. Bondy and Ross (2008) used the term "warm demanders" to describe educators who approach their students with unconditional positive regard, but simultaneously insist that their students strive to meet high academic and behavioral standards. In all four of these high-achieving schools, there were many warm demanders. Caring must be matched with an insistence that students perform to high standards. Otherwise, very little change will take place. Students and teachers may be happy, but there will be no urgency to improve. Research confirms this finding. For example, a study of middle schools in Chicago found that social support has a positive effect on academic achievement but only when coupled with a climate of strong academic press (Lee & Smith, 1999).

In addition to their own instructors, students in these schools feel they can go to any staff member for support. As one Eastlake student stated:

> No matter, like . . . I could take my English homework to my math teacher. They may not be the best teacher and know much about it, but they're willing to help. They're willing to sit down and say to you, "Let's figure this out."

Or, a junior at O'Farrell went to her freshman year teacher, when she was struggling with Advanced Placement U.S. History. She explained:

> I was really struggling with my essays . . . So I went to him three times in the morning for three essays and I would say to him, "Mr. Morgan, I kind of need help." I hadn't even talked to him all school year, and I just went to him and said, "Mr. Morgan, I need your help." And he wasn't even, like, "You need help now?" He actually sat me down and told me, "Okay, tell me about this [the essay]. I'll write everything down. I want you to make the connections yourself and you can figure out your own arguments." So he would talk to me and on all three essays, I passed with an A. He would check up on me too. In the hallways, he'd be like, "How did you do?" "I got an A." He's like, "Dude, I told you."

This openness creates an atmosphere that allows students to reach out where they are most comfortable and empowers students to take charge of their learning. All staff endeavor to minimize barriers for the students and support them to meet the high standards in place at the school.

Connecting with Colleagues

This positive, supportive culture is extended not only to students; it supports staff as well. Adults were eager to come to school. The school was a place they could learn and grow as members of a team committed to making a difference in the lives of their students. Further, staff members were empowered to work together to improve teaching and learning. As an O'Farrell teacher articulated:

> ... what keeps us going are the relationships. Not just between teachers and students but also between teachers and other teachers. . . . It's a true passion project. We want to do it, and we take initiative to start new committees or new projects that we think would benefit our students.

Teachers and other school personnel at the four schools were committed to providing the best teaching experiences for students and their relationships with their colleagues enabled them to continuously improve teaching and learning. Schools developed structures, routines, policies, and norms to build connections between teachers, as they did for student/teachers relationships. Teachers were part of collaborative teams, they observed each other's classrooms and they took responsibility for sharing knowledge and insights with each other. This created a true sense of community, characterized by a high level of trust and commitment to each other. Colleagues valued each team member, as they represented a piece of the puzzle to the school's success. We did not sense competition among educators; instead, they were more likely to share effective strategies or to seek out help from colleagues if they were struggling to reach a student or teach a concept. If a colleague asked for help, teachers did not perceive the request as a weakness. They knew their team members often had complementary strengths and were happy to provide support, as well as celebrate their colleagues' successes and learn from and with them. During one interview a teacher shared:

> We have some awesome teachers, we really do. I'm going to share something. She doesn't even know this. I'm taking a class in biliteracy for my Ph.D. and I observed her twice. I was talking to my professor about what she was doing in her class. And my professor, bilingualism is her deal. She was just amazed; she could not believe what she was getting done in there. She was using all the cutting edge research!

These relationships result is an unwavering commitment to each other, the students and the school. Pace's Dean of Instruction, Ms. Ramirez shared why she thought Pace was successful when other schools weren't, "It's our commitment, it's from the teachers, from the parents, from the students, from everybody. It's all about the commitment and the dedication that we put in this job." Establishing a school that leads so many urban students to readiness for and success in college is not easy work, but this strong foundation of a caring environment and trusting relationships helped everyone feel valued. The positive environment and trusting relationships supported a focus on continuous improvement, which helped the schools achieve excellent and equitable results for their students.

Safety and Discipline

A student code of conduct and discipline policy are integral to a well-functioning high school and contribute to the culture in implicit and explicit ways. These tools demonstrate values and beliefs about students and document expectations for behavior. When visiting each of the four schools, we immediately got a sense of those values and standards. A calm, safe, and orderly environment was evident in all schools. Safety and security were present, but they were not a dominant presence, as is often the case in urban high schools. Personnel were stationed around the large high schools, but more often than not, they were chatting and having fun with students during changing time between classes. We did not hear raised voices, harsh tones, or angry orders directed to students about what they should or should not do. One campus security representative said her job was to build relationships with students and support teachers in their classrooms. She saw her role as contributing to the safe surroundings, but also about protecting instructional time by minimizing unnecessary distractions. The primary method to achieve this was through forming relationships with both students and staff. Her partner went on further to say:

> We see ourselves in them and that's why they open up to us. And, that is how we can help them more. We understand what they are going through . . . you know, at home, and we tell them what they can do.

65

More than safe and orderly, each school was characterized by a hum of activity and purposefulness. Each school had a set of norms and values that focused everyone's attention on what was most important: engagement in school activities and learning. Students are expected to be respectful, get to class on time, be prepared, give their best effort and behave responsibly. Practices such as detention, referrals, or suspensions were available for use, but staff recognized that their use could impede student success, as it might remove students from instruction so relied far more on positive reinforcement and strong relationships.

Approaches to discipline emphasized understanding the reasons behind student behavior and educating students about the impact of their decisions. For example, at Revere High School, a member of the leadership team explained their discipline process:

> We need to find out why students are not behaving the way we want them to . . . We talk to them. We work it through with them to find out what's really driving their misbehavior and we hope to repair that. It doesn't mean we don't have consequences because we do, but we try to leverage our relationships with them to try to get them to do the right thing.

Similarly, a member of the Eastlake Leadership Team shared their perspective regarding discipline, "Discipline is a teachable moment. Kids need to know that when there is misbehavior, there is a consequence. But when you do discipline, there's a conversation. It's having a conversation because it is about having kids talk it out." He further explained, "We're trying to help them become adults." The educators know discipline is an inevitable part of the work, but it does not stand alone, it is an integral part of their student-centered culture and as such, it provides another opportunity to show students they believe in them, trust them and want the very best for them.

O'Farrell, of all of the high schools we studied, was the strictest regarding discipline, but the superintendent said, "We actually don't have to really implement it in the high school." And that was quite true; the school had extremely low referral, suspension, and expulsion numbers, while nearby high schools serving the same population of students are known for their fights and difficulty with classroom management and school safety. They may have a firm discipline policy, but it is aligned with their vision for student success, which includes character development along with postsecondary readiness. The Falcon Way and the associated behaviors are the goal for students and if they do not live up to the standard, there are consequences. The policy clearly articulates a progressive discipline approach with six or seven steps with increasing consequences if students are not demonstrating appropriate behaviors. However, students can divert the process from starting by responding and correcting the behavior after they receive a warning. Students know what is expected and can easily avoid consequences. If the process does begin and a couple of weeks pass without another incident, students go back to level one. Their goal is to empower students to make choices that are positive and aligned with their vision. They are not intending to be punitive, but rather clear about expectations and consequences with the discipline policy.

Their discipline policies are about safety and learning, rather than attempting to control student behavior through punishment. They are trying to instill self-discipline. Interestingly, at all of the schools, educators told us that students played a major role in ensuring rules were followed and the school was safe. Given the strong foundation of relationships, students were likely to go to administrators and let them know if there was an issue that needed to be addressed. This helped prevent the escalation of problems and provided opportunities for school staff to communicate with students about expectations and the reasons for the expectations. A staff member at Eastlake described:

> It's a caring community. They [students] look out for each other. If they know that somebody is not making good choices, they'll come in and tell someone because they care about their community . . . People care. They like being here. This is their second home.

And, at O'Farrell there is incentive to check up on one another. If there are no incidents at the high school, the students have free dress on Friday. Dr. Dean, the superintendent shared, "I believe the high school had free dress every Friday this year. I think all but one last year . . ."

Another common theme that emerged when discussing discipline was that administrators considered school-based factors that may contribute to negative student behaviors, in particular the quality of instruction. One assistant principal at Eastlake described:

> If our teachers are actively engaged in teaching, students will be actively engaged in learning, minimizing any classroom disruptions or behaviors. It [discipline] goes hand-in-hand with classroom instruction. As a campus, administrators provide professional development and feedback to teachers about instruction so that engagement is high in the classroom and then we do not have to deal with discipline at a high scale.

Similarly, Mr. Leal, assistant principal at Pace, said, "Students, if they're engaged, will give you good discipline, will learn, will give you their best." Proactively, administrators examine patterns in referrals and have conversations with teachers if they seem to be writing a lot of referrals to understand why it may be happening. The general practice at these schools is to look beyond the behavior to see what other factors may be at play and negatively impacting their educational goals.

Futures Full of Promise

Educators at each of the four schools shared a clear vision for the success of all of their students. The vision included success in postsecondary education, success in careers and success as a contributing member of the community. The vision included success for all students, including Latino students, English learners, recent immigrants and students who had an array of personal challenges. Teachers and other school personnel understood the implications of the vision for their everyday work life. The vision required them to know, respect and value every student and their families. The vision necessitated a belief in the capacity of each student to succeed. As well, the vision required an ability to collaborate, problem solve and create structures, routines, and norms that would maximize the likelihood of success for each student. Despite the challenges often associated with urban schools, educators were eager to do whatever was necessary to ensure each school became a place where all students learned and succeeded.

As a result, students wanted to be at these four schools. Attendance rates were far higher than typical for urban high schools (in each case exceeding 96 percent average daily attendance). Students and their parents reported that their teachers, counselors, and administrators cared about them and were committed to their immediate and long-term success. While Latino students in some schools struggle to find reasons to be hopeful about passing classes, learning foundational academic skills and graduating from high school, Latino students in these four schools acted as if their lives were full of promise, full of hope.

It is important to note that hopefulness was not achieved easily at any of the four schools. At each school, many of their Latino students had poor or mediocre grades throughout elementary and middle school and some had become known to their middle school teachers, counselors, and administrators as "behavioral problems." Many of the students entered high school far below grade level and many continued to struggle to learn English in high school. However, as these students entered Eastlake, O'Farrell, Pace, and Revere high schools they encountered teachers who acted as if they were confident that they could create the conditions that would ensure each student's success.

Despite national data trends that forecasted educational gloom for Latino students from low-income communities, educators chose to assume that their Latino students could meet eligibility criteria for college, enroll, attend, and succeed. Teachers realized that students would take different pathways to achieve college readiness, but their schools were structured to ensure all students could meet that goal. Mr. Rainey, The O'Farrell High School principal said poignantly, "Students must have the chance at the best and be expected to be the best. They're capable."

One concrete way educators helped students learn they were capable was by celebrating victories, big and small. Celebrations are a big part of these schools, from the daily announcement to pep rallies. Educators wanted students to know they noticed what students were accomplishing. Teachers and administrators wanted students to understand that they believed in their capacity to excel. They wanted students to see their own potential, engage in learning and see a positive future for themselves. For example, a math teacher at O'Farrell described how he tries to celebrate the small things and break the math into bite-sized chunks so it does not feel overwhelming, "Look you didn't even think you could do that. Look at that. Now try this one. You did that one on your own!" By structuring lessons so that students have a high likelihood of understanding one challenging concept, teachers build hope as they build students' mastery of concepts and skills. These schools are very hopeful places! Students may enter behind, but they learn that college is still in their future. Educators instill in students the belief that they are capable of changing the trajectory of their lives. Furthermore, students become convinced that their teachers will be there to support them along the way.

High Expectations for Students

To be sure, educators at these schools have high expectations. Their vision of postsecondary success for all their students is only one representation of their expectations. More importantly, the actions they take, traditions they develop and systems they implement validate this belief. This is where these four high schools differentiate themselves from other schools that also claim to have high expectations. Some high schools will challenge students with rigorous courses, stringent grading policies, strict conduct rules, and hefty homework loads. While these aspects may shape the high bar educators insist students hurdle, they may not truly reflect high expectations if educators assume that many students (or many students of color) will not reach the bar. In other words, expectations are not truly "high" unless educators can reasonably "expect" that most students will successfully achieve rigorous requirements. Otherwise, they are just standards. High schools have traditionally had standards, with the expectation that only some students would meet it and therefore be eligible for the best opportunities after high school.

When practices, programs, and policies are not aligned in ways that maximize the likelihood that students will meet challenging expectations, schools may retain a culture in which educators, parents and students expect low levels of accomplishment and high rates of failure, even though students are enrolled in rigorous courses with high standards. For example, when grades are administered on a bell curve, so only some students can do well, the grading policy signals the expectation that a significant percentage of students will fail. Similarly, if a student receives a zero grade when he does not turn in homework on time, the student's expectations of success might dwindle because of the difficulty inherent in offsetting a zero when an average of 60 or 70 is required to earn a passing grade.

Or, when a teacher is presenting a challenging academic concept, the teacher might reasonably predict that English learners will not master the concept, if the teacher presents the material through long lectures, loaded with vocabulary that will likely be unfamiliar to many students.

In contrast, in the effective schools we studied, leaders made sure that even the smallest aspects of school programs, policies, and practices contributed to the likelihood that low-income, Latino students would succeed in rigorous academic courses. Educators had high expectations for their students, but they also held high expectations for themselves. They expected themselves to adjust instructional practices, lesson designs, grading strategies, homework policies and many other practices in ways that increased the likelihood that Latino students would perceive that their academic success was likely with reasonable effort. In the next few chapters, we discuss the coherence and alignment among elements of the instructional system, so that all students achieve academic success. This coherent school design, aligned with their student-centered values, was essential to reaching their goals and ensuring all students were ready for postsecondary education and careers.

Transforming Staff Culture

The process of re-thinking programs, policies, and practices to create a culture of high expectations starts with school personnel. In the schools studied, school leaders promoted a culture of high expectations whenever they had opportunities to influence hiring decisions. These administrators strive to find and hire personnel committed to student success. Dr. Dean, superintendent at O'Farrell, has what he calls a meet and greet for 10–20 minutes with each candidate at the beginning of the hiring process. His purpose is to learn if they are committed to helping students (rather than just having a job). Further, he is looking for teachers who demonstrate a commitment to changing outcomes for historically marginalized students. Mr. Rainey, the O'Farrell Principal further explained he does not want staff to think of the students as victims. He asserted:

> If you think, "Oh, these poor kids," and therefore, "I must lower the standards because they don't have the same opportunities," That is a disservice to the students. How do

you say to somebody, "Because you've had a difficult time, I'm not going to teach you to a high standard?"

Beyond careful hiring practices, leaders influenced high expectations by promoting a culture in which educators supported each other in rethinking traditional teaching approaches. For example, teachers at Eastlake created and instituted a new motto that captured their commitment to students and demonstrated how they internalized their belief that all students could succeed: Ban the average, teach to the edges. As one teacher explained:

> The edges are everybody. There is no average student when you really look at it. In our classrooms, we really get to know our students. You could say if education was at its finest, there would be an individual educational plan for every student, right? And in essence, that's kind of what we do. We really learn who our students are. We really understand them and we really try to accommodate their needs to ensure their success.

At Eastlake, teachers set high expectations and then they work together to figure out what to do so that each and every student will be postsecondary ready. The motto was motivating to teachers and inspired them to think about their practice in new and exciting ways.

As teachers at all four schools thought about what their students needed in order to meet their high expectations, they recognized that many students needed more intensive support and intervention. However, educators at these schools tried to avoid labeling students. Students were not segregated or separated into lower-level classes focused on remediation. For example, one teacher explained the Pace approach to supporting students who needed more help. She commented, "You deal with every student like there is not going to be a barrier that is going to hold them back. You are going to work even harder. We treat the child as if there is no gap." This highly personalized approach emphasized finding and utilizing each student's strengths and interests motivating the student to learn the next important concept.

Similarly, a ninth grade math teacher at O'Farrell explained that he and his colleagues do not slow down or water down their courses when students enter high school behind academically. Instead, he explained that the O'Farrell teachers try to "meet students where they are and bridge the gap." He described how he worked with students individually and tried to understand what they knew, what they didn't know, and where the gaps were. Then he focused on addressing those gaps with additional instruction and tutoring. Johnson, Uline, and Perez (2017) described this as a positive transformational culture. Educators work together to figure out how they can transform the school by modifying their instructional strategies, homework assignments, lesson plans, other teaching practices and even their relationships with students to generate better learning results and maximize the likelihood that all students meet high academic expectations.

For students who were English learners, sometimes transforming the culture might have meant speaking in both Spanish and English in class. For a student who was highly motivated to be perceived positively by peers, it might have meant connecting the student to a small group and providing him opportunities to demonstrate an area of skill. As an Eastlake teacher articulated, "When we have our low-performing students, ESL students, or whoever it may be, we won't lower expectations. We're still expecting our students to get up here. And we'll help you get up here, but you will get up here."

Opportunities for Students

In these schools, educators try to close the gap for students and provide them with exposure and experiences they would not normally have. Educators take this responsibility seriously and opportunities range from travel, to arts, music, and sports (see Figure 3.3). Many of these opportunities take students off campus to interact with and compete with other students. As well, many of the opportunities expose students to future careers and help them learn how to pursue those interests in college and beyond. When talking with a group of seniors at Pace, we asked them about their favorite classes. Their responses pointed toward how the school was helping expose them to wide variety of options. One student was completing an internship at a doctor's office, as she was interested in the medical profession and becoming a nurse. Another student was engaged in a law practicum at the courthouse to see if she might be interested in becoming a lawyer. A third student, through the Volunteer Income Tax Assistance

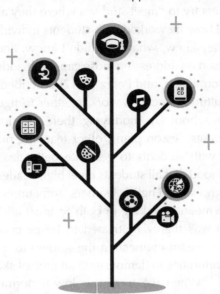

Figure 3.3 Rich and Extensive Opportunities for Students

(VITA) program, was helping community members complete their income tax returns for free every Wednesday through her business class. Another student talked about her science research and design and her forensics classes. She explained:

> Both of these courses have allowed me to open my eyes and see what's out there in the world, what I want to pursue in the future, and what I want to become. I'm not following the stereotypes that are set upon us.

As educators at all four schools envision college as a goal for their students, they also ensure they are making college attendance seem real and tangible to students. A number of the campuses utilize the Advancement Via Individual Determination (AVID) Program to help build a college-going culture, as well as take students to college fairs and do college visits. They create schedules and expectations year-by-year for what students should accomplish so they can attend college. Pace has what they call The Go Center. It is the hub for learning about and preparing for college. Students get help researching schools, completing applications and identifying and applying for scholarships. At O'Farrell, they do not use a bell system to signal the beginning and end of classes. In college, it is the students' responsibility to get to class on time, so they model and practice that in high school. As well, all students were exposed to Advanced Placement and/or dual enrollment courses to experience the rigor and structure of typical college classes. And, depending upon the school site, students were exposed to classes such as architecture, engineering, cosmetology, information technology, culinary arts, law enforcement, medical assistance, teaching, and coding. In some instances, students could receive certification in these fields while in high school. Some students saw these courses or certifications as entry points to careers they might pursue through continued study at technical schools, community colleges, or four-year universities. For other students, the courses prepared them to acquire jobs that would help them work their way through college.

Appreciation of Linguistic and Cultural Assets

Across the four schools we studied, educators cherish the diversity their students bring to school, perceiving it as an asset to be leveraged. Dr. Garcia, Revere's principal, exclaimed, "We really embrace the language they bring, the culture they bring, even the academic background they bring, and we honor those things . . . Diversity is our strength!" A member of the Revere leadership team agreed. "[We're about] respecting their culture and their language and not doing the cultural destructive model. We have to get rid of that." One concrete way Revere demonstrates this commitment is by ensuring the summer reading list each year is available in both English and Spanish. The students feel this commitment and respond to it positively. When asked their favorite thing about school, a number of students reflected on the diversity. One student explained:

> It [Revere HS] is very diverse and I always found it fascinating that so many people from so many different backgrounds all interact with each other and accept each other. You know, that's probably my favorite part of the school.

Valuing students' primary language and cultural heritage allows them to find success in their educational endeavors. It provides students with

75

the confidence to ask for support, to take advantage of new opportunities and to build confidence in their new surroundings. "I think its valuing home language," remarked a teacher at O'Farrell. "I have students in my room whose first language or home language is Spanish, and so, in class . . . there's no like—how do I say this—the world doesn't stop if someone starts speaking Spanish." Similarly, an Eastlake teacher commented:

> It helps if you are familiar with their [the students'] language and the culture because sometimes using a buzz word gets their attention. That's a big plus, when you can, because they feel more comfortable to communicate. Sometimes you take the risk and teach them in their native language. Once they pick it up, it makes it easier for them to understand the terms, because at least, now they know.

In this way, students have the opportunity to obtain clarification when struggling with academic concepts. Teachers' willingness to accommodate students' language needs allows students to both participate and process what they are learning. Research has documented that if a student's primary language foundation is strong, they make a quicker and smoother transition to their second language (Genesee, Paradise, & Crago, 2010). So, reinforcing students' understanding by building upon their culture and heritage language is one way that educators ensure everyone is included and learning. All U.S. schools take seriously the responsibility of teaching students English, but if the need should arise to use the student's native language to help students understand certain academic concepts, the educators in these exemplary schools are willing to do so. And, they reinforce to students the value of knowing two languages and maintaining and enhancing their proficiency in Spanish. One teacher at Eastlake said:

> As far as students coming in from Mexico, to high school, it's hard. But, they have to understand that they can rely on their Spanish. They have to understand that you don't leave your Spanish behind. You cannot leave your Spanish behind to learn English. Use that Spanish to be able to learn English. I think a lot of them come with the idea, "I can't learn Spanish anymore. I have to learn just English." But, knowing

two languages will help them. It will help them not only, in the U.S., it will help them if they go back to Mexico. I think that's one of the biggest things, just having them understand that you don't have to forget one language to be successful in the other."

In addition to valuing students' language, teachers also intentionally bring students' culture into lessons and activities to build pride and empower students. Some of the students feel vulnerable and they want them to feel safe and accepted at school. Sometimes, teachers accomplish this by using Spanish slang and other times it is accomplished by studying the history and culture of Mexico or the relationship between the United States and Mexico. One teacher described how she turned around a phrase her students often used that indicated they didn't know anything into a test-taking strategy. She shared:

> We try to install pride in some of the things they might say that they normally might be made fun of. So, when our kids don't know something, they say "nada que ver," which means they have no clue. So, we turn that into a test-taking strategy. As they're going over their tests, we say, "Okay, which ones are nada que ver?" Now, it's okay to say it and it's actually a powerful strategy they can use within the classroom. So we try to build on their existing language. We try to build pride and acceptance and turn what might have been considered a weakness into a strength.

Staff Role Models

Many of the educators in these schools are Latino and many of them learned English as their second language too. This provides teachers with a sense of empathy, but also reinvigorates their commitment to ensuring students master the high standards they have set. One teacher from Pace shared:

> We're not just Latinos, we are beyond that. We're each individuals and everybody has so much to offer. And I think

> if people continually put our students in that small little box with that stereotype, then what are we really doing for them?

At the four schools, various Latino staff members would share their own stories with students to reinforce that although it may feel overwhelming, the future is likely to be quite positive. One staff member reflected,

> . . . being here is completely different than being in Mexico. Knowing that people understand is helpful . . . I was a second-language learner and so when students come to me I'm able to understand and empathize. And when I say, "You want to learn English? Let's work on it," students feel supported.

Similarly, another staff member said:

> The students see people who maybe have similar backgrounds as them who are successful, who have forged a path, made decisions and learned life lessons that they're now transferring over to them. The students see the benefit. They see a light at the end of the tunnel that they might not have seen previously.

There have been recent calls to diversify the teacher workforce to better serve students of color, who are quickly becoming the majority in public schools. Research on matching students and teachers race and ethnicity is emerging and showing benefits for students in regard to perceptions of ability and academic outcomes (Dee, 2004, 2005; Egalite & Kisida, 2017; Egalite, Kisida, & Winters, 2015). One hypothesis of how this occurs is students can see their teachers as role models (Goldhaber, Theobold, & Tien, 2015). Here we can see and experience the value that emerges in interactions and student experiences. Both students and teachers feel positive about what they are doing and accomplishing.

Just as Latino teachers, administrators and other school personnel were important role models, at the four schools studied, educators realized that peers could be powerful role models, as well. At Pace, they have a College Wall that shows where all of the seniors are going after graduation plus it showcases students who are taking college courses/dual enrollment.

They believe this "gives the other students encouragement regarding where they can go and what they can shoot for."

Support for Bilingual Learners

In addition to valuing and including students' native language in regular instruction, each school accommodated the English language development needs of their Latino students into the overall instructional system. Each school had a different percentage of English learners and these learners were on a continuum of proficiency, which necessitated varying levels of intervention and support. But, the main goal was that they acquire the academic language and proficiency to be able make any choice they wanted after high school. For instance, at Pace, Ms. Longoria shared the following:

> . . . some of our students take additional English classes. So, we need to give them that extra, extra support. For our English language learners, we provide English labs and an ELL instructional aid that works directly with them. We also have a specialized teacher that runs the Language Learners at University of Texas at Austin's Center for Hispanic Acheivement lab (LUCHA) which also serves as a Latino student support group.

At Pace, extra English classes are provided for the English Learner students to develop their reading and writing skills so students can effectively engage in higher-level academic content classes. Teachers provide extra English courses within the mixed, nine-period/block schedule to still allow space in students' schedules for electives and other core courses. They want students to remain on track to graduate and explore their interests. Pace strives to support students in moving as quickly as possible from one level to the next, so students can meet the same educational goals as other students.

At Revere High School, the teachers shared that recently arrived English Learners were referred to the Newcomers Academy to immerse them into their second language to build their proficiency. A teacher explained:

> . . . for English learners, some students are coming in way below grade level, so we have a Newcomers Academy. . . . We have teachers who are trained to teach students so that they have the foundational skills as they move into level one. We also have summer English learner programs.

Additionally, Revere students have access to English learner classes after school. Between summer school and after school hours, newcomers have maximum opportunities to develop English skills, while they are developing the academic skills that will be essential to their post-secondary success.

At The O'Farrell High School, English learner students are part of the mainstream campus with in-classroom support. The aide described her work in this way:

> We're making sure that the students are engaged and learning. We go to the classes, making sure that the students understand what the teacher is teaching. We translate a lot of the time because most of our students do not speak English yet. We translate. We run a club after school, making sure that students are doing their homework. We make phone calls to our parents, making sure that the students are understanding the subject.

The instructional coach at O'Farrell further explained how their model of in-classroom support was designed:

> It's just immersed, so you're not going to go into an ELL wing or the ELL portable trailer. It is just immersed. We're actually getting ready for an audit and one of the questions is how we designate the qualifications of the teacher who teaches ELLs and we're sort of giggling because every teacher interacts with ELLs. A teacher who interacts with ELLs just means an O'Farrell teacher.

As a result, at O'Farrell a portion of professional development is specifically focused on English learner strategies. They know the strategies are good for all students and help everyone access the curriculum. This year, because of their efforts, they reclassified a number of students and were feeling positively about the results and students' readiness for high-level classes including Advanced Placement.

Conclusion

> Our administration is 100 percent student focused. If there is something that is going to benefit the student, they will find the money and spend it. If there is some kind of problem with the student, they will stop everything to make sure those students' needs are met. Emotionally, academically or whatever. We will sit down and if it takes us all day to do, we'll go through every students' name and talk about each student individually.
>
> —Eastlake Teacher

Like many prior reforms in education, "being student-centered" has become the current en vogue idea and lots of schools are trying to improve their practice in this area. However, like lots of reforms in education, there is often a lack of clarity about what this means and various terms are used further complicating understanding (e.g., student-centered, personalized learning, deeper learning, learner-centered education). Lists have been created about what teachers should do in their classrooms (e.g., let students choose projects/what they will study, how they will study it and how they will demonstrate their knowledge) or methods they should use (e.g. collaboration, project-based learning, differentiated instruction, etc.). The four high schools we profile demonstrate it is not as simple as lists and practices to adopt. Rather, educators created a pervasive sense that students are the focus and instruction, curriculum, leadership, and services coalesce around ensuring students learn and succeed and the same high expectations and goals are held for every student. This commitment centers on ensuring students and their families feel valued, capable, and respected, which research has documented is especially important for Latino students, who have historically been marginalized in schools. In these schools, Latino and English learner students' culture and language was viewed as an asset and was incorporated seamlessly into school operations. The acceptance of culture and language did not lead to lower expectations or alternate standards. Relationships are at the core of these schools and it is within this context that students are challenged academically and are helped to identify their strengths and talents and what they need to do to accomplish their dreams. These exemplary schools also seek out new opportunities for students to experience and expand their range of options. "What is in the best interest of the students?" was the guiding question as educators sought to transform their schools to ensure the success of each and every student.

Self-Assessment

1) How would you articulate the core values at your school?
   a) Are they student-centered?
   b) Are they comprehensive and aligned with your vision?

2) What evidence suggests that students and families feel welcomed and valued at your school?
   a) If your evidence is lacking, what steps could you take to improve the culture?
   b) If your evidence is strong, what steps can you take to sustain this atmosphere?

3) Are there groups of students who are less likely to feel welcomed and valued at your school?
   a) Which groups of students are least likely to feel welcomed and valued?
   b) Which groups of parents are least likely to feel welcomed and valued?
   c) What can be done to maximize the likelihood that all students and parents feel welcomed and valued?

4) What systems or practices are in place to provide opportunities for staff and students to get to know each other?

5) What opportunities allow school personnel to work collaboratively together and get to know one another across departments and grades?

6) Would you say you have provided your students with educational opportunities that expose and prepare them for higher education or future work environments?

a) Create a list of these opportunities and examine how comprehensive it is. Is anything missing? Are some things overrepresented?

b) Which students get access to these experiences? Are there barriers for some groups of students? What can be done to mitigate these barriers?

7) What is your approach to discipline?

a) How does it reflect your school values?

b) Do all students feel physically and emotionally safe at school?

c) Do all school personnel feel physically and emotionally safe at school?

d) Is discipline implemented consistently by all staff and for all students?

e) Are students more or less likely to feel welcomed and valued after receiving discipline or correction?

f) Do you have a system to identify trends in discipline issues?

8) In what ways do you demonstrate that you value the home language and culture of your students?

a) What support does your school provide to help students build their bilingual strengths or share their heritage at school?

b) How are expectations communicated to teachers, students, and parents?

References

Bazron, B., Osher, D., & Fleischman, S. (2005). Creating culturally responsive schools. *Educational Leadership, 63*(1), 83–84.

Bondy, E., & Ross, D. D. (2008). The teacher as warm demander. *Educational Leadership, 66*(1), 54–58.

Dee, T. S. (2004). Teachers, race, and student achievement in a randomized experiment. *The Review of Economics and Statistics, 86*, 195–210.

Dee, T. S. (2005). A teacher like me: Does race, ethnicity, or gender matter? *American Economic Review, 95*, 158–65.

Egalite, A. J., Kisida, B., & Winters, M. A. (2015). Representation in the classroom: The effect of own-race teachers on student achievement. *Economics of Education Review, 45*, 44–52.

Egalite, A. J., & Kisida, B. (2017). The effects of Teacher Match on students' academic perceptions and attitudes. *Educational Evaluation and Policy Analysis, 18*, 1–23.

Gándara, P., R. Rumberger, J. Maxwell-Jolly, & R. Callahan. (2003). English learners in California schools: Unequal resources, unequal outcomes. *Educational Policy Analysis Archives, 11*(36), 1–52.

García, S. B., & Guerra, P. L. (2004). Deconstructing deficit thinking: Working with educators to create more equitable learning environments. *Education and Urban Society 36*(2), 150–68.

Genesee, F., Paradis, J., & Crago (Eds.) (2010). *Dual language development and disorders: A handbook on bilingualism and second language learning* (2nd edition). Baltimore, MD: Brookes Publishing.

Goldhaber, D., Theobald, R., & Tien, C. (2015). *Theoretical and empirical arguments for diversifying the teacher workforce: A review of the evidence* (CEDR Policy Brief No. 2015–920159). Retrieved from www.cedr.us/papers/working/CEDR%20WP%202015-9.pdf

Johnson, J. F., Uline, C. L., & Perez, L. G. (2017). *Leadership in America's best urban schools.* New York: Routledge.

Lee, V. E., & Smith, J. B. (1999). Social support and achievement for young adolescents in Chicago: The role of school academic press. *American Educational Research Journal, 36*(4), 907–45.

Rolon, C. (2005). Succeeding with Latino Students. *Principal, 85*(2), 30–34.

Implementing High-Powered Curricula, Strategies, and Programs

The biggest thing about working together is the fact that instruction will go on with or without you. I know that if I'm absent tomorrow, my team will pick it up . . . Nothing will stop instruction. Nothing. Instruction will go on, no matter what. And that has got to be the message. No matter what, it's going to continue. It's going to continue with or without you. Tomorrow is going to come. The sun will rise up and instruction must go on.

—*Teacher, Pace High School*

Not long ago, high schools were organized to ensure that the very brightest students were challenged with a rigorous curriculum that would prepare them for college. Another group of students would get foundational academic material to provide them access to less selective colleges or open access community colleges, and still another group of students would hopefully make it to high school graduation, meeting minimum standards, and gaining general skills so that they were employable. These tracks, or ability groups, often mirrored the demographic characteristics of students, with the low and middle tracks largely comprising low-income students and students of color (Oakes & Guiton, 1995). Still today, despite the rhetoric of college and career readiness for all students, recent data show eight percent of high school graduates complete a full college and career preparatory curriculum and nearly half of students complete neither a college nor career preparatory curriculum (Bromberg & Theokas, 2016). The data suggest high schools are offering a number of different curriculum pathways from vocational to college prep and students meander towards graduation, accruing credits rather than experiencing a cohesive curriculum that prepares them to pursue their goals after high school.

The high schools profiled in this book are quite different. Yes, they provide a number of curricular opportunities for students, but a very different mission guides them and organizes their work. Their goal is to ensure all students get the same quality education most middle and high-income students receive, including honors and advanced classes with deep learning and meaningful engagement that develops their critical thinking skills and personal interests. These educators know not all of their students will go to college, but, they strive to ensure that every student will be prepared to succeed in college if they choose to attend. As one student explained:

> They say, "we're not here to force you guys to go to college. We're here to make sure you guys are ready for college, and in case you choose not to go, you have a back-up plan." You're still prepared for it [college] though.

Leaders and educators in these schools know that educational systems have often failed students from low-income communities (and particularly low-income, Latino students), so they passionately endeavor to ensure that each student succeeds. "Every kid on this planet has the same value and the same worth. And every kid deserves the same education," the principal of O'Farrell asserted. "It doesn't matter where you grow up. It doesn't matter what your last name is. It doesn't matter what you look like or whether you have a dad at home or not. Every kid deserves the same education." The other three principals echoed this same sentiment. For example, the Pace principal, Mrs. Longoria, reflected on her experience in high school. She explained that as a senior, math was not required, and her parents were unaware that such a course would be helpful as she moved on to college. Since she was not viewed as "college going," no one at the school counseled her to enroll in a math course in her senior year, and, as a result, she struggled in college. She emphasized that she wants her students to be prepared when they go to college, so nothing will derail them.

Teachers at the four schools articulated the same commitment to ensuring that their students had access to quality curricula. For example, one teacher bluntly said, "The biggest thing is that you have got to stop thinking that they are Latinos, or they are whatever. If it is a student, I will teach them the same material. In my case—Algebra I. It is about student success." Educators at these high schools refused to let negative stereotypes or low expectations change their focus. They are intent on ensuring their students receive the same rigorous instruction as other students.

At all four schools, educators perceived high school graduation as only a step toward their real goal of ensuring that each student was ready to succeed in postsecondary education. While educators at many schools talk about preparing all students for postsecondary education, at these four high schools, they measure their progress toward the goal with an external standard, that is, earning Advanced Placement (AP) or dual-enrollment credits and/or achieving a qualifying score on a college readiness test (e.g., SAT, ACT or, in Texas, the Texas Success Initiative (TSI) Assessment). The data indicate all four high schools are doing well. For example, at Revere HS, 42 percent of seniors took at least one AP test and the students earned a passing score on 62 percent of the AP tests they took. Similarly, about 68 percent of students at O'Farrell take an AP course by their senior year, which places them in the top 7 percent of high schools in California. AP, International Baccalaureate (IB), or Cambridge courses are a powerful means of disrupting high-end achievement gaps, but national data document that many students miss out on these opportunities (Theokas & Saaris, 2013). Nationally, only about 12 percent of each graduating class participates in AP. Although the four schools, on average, have far greater participation, none of the school leaders were satisfied. Most of the principals said one of their goals was to increase advanced course participation and passing rates. This self-imposed accountability led educators to build a system (including structures, supports, routines and norms) that would increase the likelihood that every student would have access to challenging curricula and effective instruction that would prepare them to succeed in postsecondary academic pursuits. This system includes three essential elements discussed in this chapter:

1. the master schedule—the framework that guides high school offerings,

2. the guaranteed and viable curriculum, made accessible to all students through the collaborative planning of first (or initial) instruction, and

3. the intervention and enrichment strategies that surround first instruction to ensure each student's unique needs, strengths/weaknesses

and interests are supported (Johnson, Uline, & Perez, 2017; Marzano, et al., 2005).

These three components are interdependent, but all must be individually addressed with fidelity to ensure that all students learn, make progress, and are prepared to succeed in postsecondary education upon graduation.

The students in these four high schools are provided the opportunity to learn the same standards pursued by students in middle-class communities in their states. Students perceive that classroom instruction is meaningful and relevant to their backgrounds and to their futures, and a rich system of support ensures mastery. In this chapter, we share commonalities in how educators in the four schools ensured a rigorous curriculum and set and maintained high expectations. We also describe how educators have developed and adapted processes to the unique context of their school, given variability in size, resources, and student needs and interests. The following chapters focuses on the systems that support excellent instruction of the curriculum: Observation/Feedback & Support, Professional Development, and Using Data to Track and Monitor Progress, Improvement and Success. Figure 4.1 shows all the elements of the coherent school design- a key practice identified in our research. These systems push students to excel and support both teachers and students to reach their full potential.

Figure 4.1 Coherent and Aligned Educational Systems

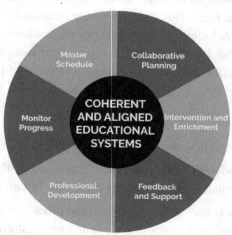

First Things First: The Master Schedule

Anyone who has worked in a high school knows the horror of constructing a master schedule: the framework that allocates minutes, resources, and staffing to help the school achieve its mission. It articulates who teaches what, when, and where. (It also determines who accesses what, when and if they access it at all!) Creating individual schedules for hundreds or thousands of students, managing the contractual rules concerning how many periods a teacher can instruct, ensuring that students and teachers will have ample opportunities to eat lunch and responding to demands for courses as varied as AP Calculus to art, band, foreign language, career and technical education classes and internships is a daunting assignment. In typical high schools, the architects of the master schedule tend to prioritize adult needs and desires. For example, the most experienced teachers are assigned to teach the most academically advanced students and often have the smallest class sizes. All students who take the same course are expected to learn class content at the same time, after the same number of minutes of instruction. Once established, the master schedule is rarely altered because of the impact of changes on the workloads of administrators, counselors, and teachers. (Murray, 2011). Typically, students are scheduled in large batches, with little attention to individual needs and preferences. Often, students are winners or losers in acquiring seats in classes that best meet their needs.

Master Schedule Models

While there are a number of secondary school scheduling models (i.e., traditional period, block, modified block, 75–75–30), research does not support one model over another, but rather indicates the best approach to schedule choice involves building consensus over priorities, defining goals and engaging stakeholders in determining the best method to reach such goals (Hanover Research, 2014; Zepada and Mayers, 2006). During our visits to each of the high schools, we learned that not only did each school change their schedule model at some point, but also that the placement of students in classes and the schedule itself were fluid. Principals did not hesitate to accommodate teacher wishes. As the Pace principal explained,

> Oh my god. . . the master schedule, you know, making sure that every child is in the right place at the right time. Also, allowing the teachers to manipulate that, to come in and say, "This is what I want. Move this class here. Move this kid . . ."

Student needs were also at the forefront. As a Pace counselor explained, "If a student does not like one class, it can ruin their whole day and make them not want to be here. So, we change it. We don't penalize kids. We try to find what they are interested in."

The master schedule at these high schools reveals their true beliefs, attitudes, values and priorities. As a team, they create the master schedule and adjust it to the needs of their students. In contrast, at some schools, administrators, or counselors squeeze students into open slots as if they expect students to adjust. Attention to the needs of students makes the work of those in charge of the master schedule more difficult, but educators at the four schools studied seemed eager to do so because they recognized how important scheduling was to ensure the success of each student.

Pace Early College High School

When Rose Longoria arrived at Pace, she encountered academic challenges, but she saw promise.

> I saw potential when I got here. This is going to be great. I'm always open to a challenge. I knew that if we were here, we could only go up. It was going to be a challenge to get the accolades [achieved by other schools in the district], but it was possible.

She was determined to fight for the school and take advantage of opportunities she saw to better meet the needs of the students. She recognized that by changing how the master schedule was constructed and by changing what the schedule contained, she could advance Pace toward excellent learning outcomes for all students.

The Brownsville Independent School District allows leaders at each high school to choose their master schedule model. Pace staff decided to implement a modified-block schedule with three eight-period days of roughly 55 minutes and two four-period days of 90-minutes. This allowed each teacher to have his or her students for one extended period each week. During these longer lessons, students apply what they had learned earlier in the week through hands-on activities, labs and debates. During our interviews, students spontaneously described the benefits of having such a schedule. "[We can] . . . study a little deeper into the topic for a longer time. You get a different type of perspective doing that." The students also noted that the longer periods were more similar to what they would experience in college and that this provided them the opportunity to practice managing their attention and participating effectively. Interestingly, the students also recognized that the schedule helped them with time management of their workload. During block days, they could "compartmentalize and focus" on only a few subjects. Of course, it was also nice that they only had to carry four books around, as well!

One challenge the administrators noted with the modified-block schedule was that it worked best with one lunch period. However, it can be quite challenging for a large high school to move 2,000 students through the lunch line in one lunch period with adequate supervision. Nonetheless, Pace leaders determined that it was important for them to maximize the effectiveness of their modified-block schedule by keeping only one lunch period. They considered their priorities and made choices to ensure a safe lunch. In particular, they did not want to compromise their commitment to support excellence in teaching and learning, so they chose for teachers to not have assigned duty during lunch. Consequently, the administrative team took over lunchtime supervision. The students are respectful of the time and it runs smoothly. Students were observed waiting patiently in line, hanging out with friends in different sitting areas, cleaning up and going right to class when the bell rang. Teachers appreciated that they did not need to supervise students during lunch period. They could devote their full attention and energy to their classes.

After choosing the modified-block schedule, the Pace leadership team realized that the structure for providing students enrichment and/or intervention was not sufficient for students. Students were limited in their access to electives and some students needed more time for intensive instruction (in particular, English language development). So, they adjusted time allocations and moved from an eight- to a nine-period day. This extra period allowed some students to accelerate their learning and take additional classes, (e.g., dual enrollment) and/or receive intervention without limiting their access to electives or important core classes. Students can still take electives and graduate with the credit they need to be prepared for postsecondary options. Pace educators were adamant that the master schedule should allow students to receive the extra support they needed, while they still enjoyed access to a broad, rich curriculum.

The leadership team also realized the schedule needed to be coordinated to maximize collaboration for teachers if they wanted to meet their goals. The district required that each teacher have two planning periods per day. At Pace, teachers in the same subject and department share both planning periods. Mrs. Longoria reflected that it was a "nightmare" to get both planning periods coordinated for teachers but the administrative team wanted to make it as easy as possible for teachers to work together, plan and support each other. This scheduling feature minimizes the need for teachers to work after school or on the weekends and maximizes opportunities for teachers to build upon each other's curricular and instructional strengths. To further facilitate this collaboration, teachers who teach the same course teach next door or across the hall from one another.

In addition, Pace High School created labs and tutorials before school, after school and on Saturdays for students in need of intervention to supplement the master schedule. Of course, some students could not attend tutorials at the scheduled times because of their other responsibilities (e.g., getting siblings to school or working part-time jobs to help support their family). This required further master schedule adjustments to accommodate some tutorials during the school day. Ultimately, the Pace staff was willing to do whatever it took in order for their students to succeed.

Revere High School

At Revere High School, educators chose a different master schedule model; however, their decision was driven by a similar focus on improving student success. Dr. Garcia came at a time when change was needed in order to take the school to a higher level of student success. The superintendent of the Revere Public Schools stated:

> We needed somebody who didn't have formal relationships
> with all of the high school teachers . . . We needed somebody
> who could come in with his or her own perspective and

even bring perspectives from other successful school districts and teach us to move forward from where we were at at that time. So, Doc came on, and we let him take over.

Throughout the years, the demographics at Revere High School had changed drastically. The student population grew from 1,500 to 1,800 and continues to grow as the city experiences a new wave of immigration. As Dr. Garcia explained, "Every day we get two, three, four, or five kids coming. Most of the kids are coming from Latin American countries. We have 30 languages spoken in the school." Both the superintendent and principal were committed to continuing their focus on the 4Rs: rigor, relationships, resiliency and relevance. They wanted these priorities to be reflected in the master schedule to ensure all students would benefit. They knew that the former schedule was not conducive to rigorous teaching and learning. They decided that changing from a seven-period traditional schedule to a four-period block schedule would improve rigor and student learning in the classroom. In addition, they built in a 24-minute advisory period, three days per week to address the relationship component of the 4Rs. They wanted teachers and students to have more time get to know one another better, build trust, and form strong bonds that would last beyond high school. The students at Revere responded well to the new master schedule. In the words of one student, "I like longer blocks because you get to take core classes early on, and then you can take more electives and do internships later in your career." Or, according to another student, "With fewer classes at one time, it allows you to focus more. It also allows for more electives so that you can explore your interests and prepare for what you might want to do after you leave high school."

Advisory was scheduled for three days per week, which left open two 39-minute periods per week that are devoted to teacher learning. Teachers meet in small "professional learning groups" (PLGs) to discuss best practices, examine student work, talk about the progress a student is making in one class that is not matched in another class and, generally, to align their work. The PLG meetings are typically departmental, but once per month they meet cross-departmentally to facilitate alignment across the curriculum. These meetings are peer led discussions on diverse topics. The idea is to support regular communication and build safe spaces for colleagues to become "critical friends" to support the ongoing improvement of teaching and learning.

The transition to this new schedule had its challenges. First, it had to be put to a vote in order to make the change and the block schedule did not receive landslide support. Dr. Garcia mentioned the conversation he had with the superintendent as they were counting the votes, "'Well, you got 49 percent to 51 percent. So, you have your mandate.' I remember those [the Superintendent's] words. We knew there was a problem. It was tight, and we had a lot of work to do around the change." They both knew teacher buy-in was key in order to make the change successful. Dr. Kelly, the superintendent, reflected, "The teachers have to buy-in and in order for them to buy-in, they have to have a voice in the decision making." So, the Revere leadership team began a series of conversations with their teachers to get their feedback and also share their thoughts about why this was a priority for the school. As a result of these conversations, two decisions were made: 1) Teachers would have a full block devoted to common planning where they could analyze student assignments and data with their colleagues and 2) professional development, the first year, would focus on the skills teachers needed to engage students for the full period. The students were not accustomed to sitting for 80 minutes, and the teachers were not in the habit of planning for that length of time. To increase the effectiveness of the professional development, it was complemented with ongoing support in the classrooms. This provided teachers immediate feedback, modeling, and opportunities to try new things with support. Teachers also visited more effective teachers' class-rooms to observe what they were doing to maximize the impact of instructional time. Dr. Garcia said changing the master schedule was a monumental task but, without the changes, he believed their students would not be college and career ready within the four years. It was not an easy transition, but support was strategically crafted in order to make the change successful and benefit students.

The O'Farrell High School and Eastlake High School

O'Farrell and Eastlake also made changes to their master schedule models to meet the learning needs of their students. Eastlake follows a hybrid year-round calendar and opens early each morning with a "zero period" and closes around 7p.m. for students who have a ninth period or tutorial. And, just last year, O'Farrell switched to a modified-block schedule, with four block-period days and one day during which students experience all of their classes. At both schools, the change to the master schedule was purposeful. Educators knew what they wanted to accomplish, they researched options, made the changes, and then did everything they could to ensure the change was successful for students and helped the school achieve its goals.

Incorporating Students' Interests

In all four schools, changes to the master schedule created the organizational framework for teaching and learning. With the framework in place, all four school leaders let student interests drive curricular offerings and opportunities. For example, Eastlake prides itself on offering opportunities that include "something for everyone." As one Eastlake educator explained:

> I think it's just giving students the opportunity to pursue what they are passionate about. We have lots of courses in different career paths where they get to actually choose and take what they're interested in. Regardless, they are still expected to meet the requirements that every other student needs to meet, but they get to do something they are passionate about.

At Eastlake there are opportunities to explore the culinary arts, biomedical sciences, engineering, aerospace, cosmetology, and veterinary medicine. In the School of Advanced Technology Applications (SATA), students learn to be computer scientists and have coursework in application, video game, and website development. A full complement of athletic and arts opportunities are offered. Eastlake also provides dual enrollment classes during the school year and summer, where students can experience college life by taking classes at the local community college. The wide array of curricular offerings helps ensure that all students can pursue their passions.

As discussed in Chapter Two, Eastlake is a relatively new school (six years) with a brand new facility and capacity to serve 3,000 students. The school was still under construction as the first ninth grade class arrived.

Mr. Martinez had the opportunity to influence how space was utilized as he got to know the students and they began advocating for their interests. Currently, the campus has an industrial kitchen, theater spaces, fields, dance studios, band and mariachi rooms, and kennels and runs for animals cared for in the veterinary program. There are still some unused spaces, so it will be interesting to see how they decide to use them!

In contrast, O'Farrell serves about 500 high school students on a small, tight campus with some facilities shared with the elementary and middle school. The small physical space, however, does not limit the opportunities for students. It just takes a different form, as student engagement and exposure are priorities, just like at other large comprehensive high schools. Dr. Dean's philosophy when starting O'Farrell was "whatever the kids need." Like Eastlake, O'Farrell recently graduated its first class, but unlike Eastlake it did not start in a new building; they initially borrowed four classrooms from The O'Farrell Middle School to house their first ninth grade class. Soon, the school was a hallway on the middle school campus. Eventually, they needed and were able to build their own space. The O'Farrell High School now proudly sits on the "upper campus" and has its own office, classroom wings (named for different colleges) and an auditorium. Future plans include creating fields for athletic games.

As the high school was being developed, the teachers realized that it was important for students to have a full high school experience and petitioned the California Interscholastic Federation to offer sports their first year. With only about 100 students and a requirement to offer sports for both boys and girls on eight different teams, it was not easy. But, teachers convinced lots of students that they should play some sport. Mr. Rainey, who became the principal, coached track the first couple of years. A banner commemorates their winning season that first year- with only five girls! One year, the girls' soccer team disappeared as they didn't have enough students, but as soon as enough students were interested, the team came back.

To offer O'Farrell students a full complement of experiences, Mr. Rainey encouraged classroom teachers to teach electives and run afterschool clubs. And the O'Farrell teachers are all in. When students initiate a new club idea, teachers offer to be the teacher of record. And, when exploring ideas for additional electives, Mr. Rainey explained, "I go to teachers and say, 'What do you love that you could teach as an elective?' And then one teacher says, 'I love photography.' And I say, 'Let's teach photography.' and you know we do it!" So, every teacher teaches some

Figure 4.2 Features of the Master Schedule

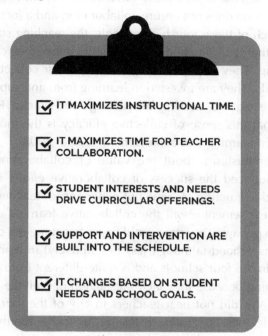

- ☑ IT MAXIMIZES INSTRUCTIONAL TIME.
- ☑ IT MAXIMIZES TIME FOR TEACHER COLLABORATION.
- ☑ STUDENT INTERESTS AND NEEDS DRIVE CURRICULAR OFFERINGS.
- ☑ SUPPORT AND INTERVENTION ARE BUILT INTO THE SCHEDULE.
- ☑ IT CHANGES BASED ON STUDENT NEEDS AND SCHOOL GOALS.

kind of elective. Now, with four grades and 500 students, O'Farrell has added a full-time theater teacher and next year will add a full-time music teacher. O'Farrell educators found ways to engage their students in loving learning by teaching them what they loved. And little by little, the electives developed and were adapted and changed based on student interests and needs. Figure 4.2 highlights the essential features of the master schedule.

Collaboration for Effective Instruction

With the master schedule set and with multiple opportunities for students to explore their interests, each of the schools focused on what occurs in classes to ensure student mastery is achieved. Educators at all four high schools tried to ensure that every child, in every class, was being exposed to the same content and essential skills and was learning the same challenging academic standards, no matter who their teacher was. This is accomplished a number of different ways. The master schedule ensures teachers who teach the same content have the same planning periods, but common time alone does not ensure collaboration and a focus on student learning. In each of these four high schools, the teaching staff aspires to be masters of their practice and believe that together they can influence student learning. They rely on one another and their collective efforts to reach their goals. They are invested in learning from and supporting each other to ensure that no student falls through the cracks. Research has documented that this sense of collective efficacy is the most influential factor in student learning and achievement (Hattie, 2008).

Teacher enthusiasm about the value of collaborating with their colleagues influenced the success of collaborative efforts in improving curriculum and instruction. A new, but experienced, teacher at O'Farrell expressed his excitement about the collaborative learning environment. "You'll have to pry away my dead, cold finger to get me out of here!" This enthusiasm was echoed (although less descriptively) in many interviews with teachers in the four schools and is quite different from stories about teachers resigning because they lack satisfaction or feel like robots rather than teachers. We did not hear teachers in any of the four schools talk about scripted lessons, an oppressive testing culture, or punitive evaluation systems (common reasons for dissatisfaction in more typical urban schools). Instead, teachers described their work as a "passion project," "intellectually engaging" and "not like work." Teachers also described themselves as, professionals. They are striving to be experts and it is through their collective work with their colleagues that they believe they will get there. According to one teacher:

> Administrators, teachers and the students are all collaborating toward a shared goal of helping our kids to get in and through college or to and through some sort of post-high school plans where they are committed and are successful. We all share that vision. We're given a voice and we are able to exercise creative liberties to achieve that goal.

Teacher Accountability

These teachers feel enormous responsibility for their students' learning and success in life. They don't feel alone or like they are searching in the dark for answers. We believe both of these elements are important. Being part of a group is insufficient; the group must have an effective strategy for defining clearly what students need to learn, determining methods for gauging student success, identifying and considering pedagogical alternatives, trying approaches that have the greatest likelihood of success, collecting and reviewing implementation data, and refining those practices until students achieve the desired learning results. Educators don't get it right all the time, but the system allows them to make midcourse corrections and successive approximations to their goals. And, because they collaborate with colleagues about which standards to teach and share common formative assessments to check if students learned the material, they can also see when colleagues achieve or don't achieve success.

The commitment teachers felt to their colleagues powerfully influenced the quality of teacher collaboration. When there is lack of commitment, it is easy to say, "We did that. It didn't work." It is far more demanding to reflect on why. It was not uncommon for teachers to tell us they talk to their colleagues in the hallway in between classes to get feedback when something didn't go the way they planned in their class and to hear how successful their partner teachers were with implementation. At O'Farrell, teachers even felt like their students were part of the feedback process. As teachers, they knew when a lesson flopped, so did the students! In this case, teachers might ask the students, how can we do things differently and better? As one teacher described:

> I really feel like my students are part of my team. We are all working towards the same goal. I think about my AP class for example. We are all there, we are working and I am helping them and they are helping me. We are growing together and we're in it, really in it together.

PLCs or professional learning communities are ubiquitous in public education and have been on the leading edge of reform for a number of years. One estimate suggests that 90 percent of schools set aside some time each week for teachers to work together. And, indeed, research indicates that effective PLCs can and do change teacher practice and student learning outcomes (Vescio et al., 2007). However, in many schools, we have witnessed "PLCs" where, although teachers are in the same room, they are not even sitting together, looking at, or talking to one another. Another variation is a group of teachers sitting together with an agenda, but conversations focus on complaints about students, parents, administrators and generally everything about the job other than instruction. Conversations meander, rather than support the collective learning of the group. Sometimes, we find some teachers working together, looking at student work and some teachers disengaged from the process. In typical schools, there is little teacher-to-teacher effort to share challenges, best practices, or to support one another's growth, even though they may claim some elements of a PLC structure. In all of these cases, there was some restructuring of the schedule and time, but not enough "re-culturing." According to Fullan (2000), it takes approximately three years for an elementary and six years for a high school to achieve successful change in practice and student performance. This points to the fact that we need adoption and implementation, as well as strong institutionalization of new practices to move toward real and meaningful change that improves student outcomes. In Chapter Five, we will discuss the school goals each school had and how they focused on a small set of practices each year to ensure they achieved efficacy and implementation.

Assessment

In the schools we visited, pedagogy and assessment feed each other, through the interaction of teachers during formal and informal collaborations among colleagues. During PLC meetings, teachers study the standards, design lessons and units together and build common formative assessments. In addition, they examine student work to assess the impact of instruction. When visiting Pace, we had the opportunity to observe the U.S. History teachers during their collaboration. The two-teacher team had been teaching together for some time. They had a process, which included coming in over the summer to write the curriculum and then planning daily to see what was working and what accommodations needed to be made based on their students and classrooms. When we walked in, they each had their students' interactive notebooks stacked up next to them and they were reviewing how students approached and completed the day's assignment in each of their classrooms. On this day, they noted very similar results across classrooms. Student work seemed superficial with facts and knowledge, but the students did not connect the facts to the larger concepts of the emerging American identity and ideas about independence and equality. Stylistically, these two teachers were very different in their classrooms, but they observed very similar results. They realized they needed to do something different instructionally. In particular, they decided they needed to build more time in for student discussion as what they had done to date focused too much on teacher instruction. They began creating some new lessons that featured questions for students to grapple with in small groups. These new questions would encourage students to analyze historical contexts and apply the concepts they were learning.

In addition to reviewing assessment results and student work, these two teachers also expect students to track their own data. The stated goal for students is 80 percent mastery (the state test requires 32 percent) and they expect the students to improve on each assessment over the course of the year. They believe this helps engage students and helps them to participate and make choices regarding their learning.

The algebra teachers at Pace are a much larger group of six, with a couple of new members and some with more experience working with each other and with the students at Pace. During their PLC, they were reviewing results from their most recent benchmark assessment. The state test (required for graduation) was approaching. The teachers believed 100 percent of their students would pass and the purpose of their planning was to ensure they achieved what they believed was possible. Based on their assessments of the students, the teachers were moving cards (each card had a student's name) into different tiers (red, yellow, and green). A number of students remained in the red, but "it was fewer than last year." They reflected on some of the changes they made that likely produced these results. In particular, the teachers credited their DEED motto (do everything, every day) approach with their success in reducing the number of students in the red tier. This means focusing on all the state standard strands (linear, quadratic, translations, etc.) in each lesson. They had spent a lot of time really understanding the standard strands and planning how to incorporate each strand into their lessons and what level of assessment was necessary to provide feedback about student mastery.

As the algebra teachers planned their approach for the next five weeks, they thought about what they needed to do differently for the students in the red tier and what was important to ensure the continued growth of students in the yellow and green tiers. The teachers decided they would move students between classrooms to ensure instruction was targeted to each student's needs. When observing algebra classrooms later in the week, we witnessed teachers working on the same standard, albeit quite differently. In one classroom, there was a strong emphasis on vocabulary and the teacher moved between English and Spanish to ensure students were acquiring the terminology and its relationship to the mathematical processes. Another classroom was focusing on the sequence of steps to solve the problem and using the graphing calculator to understand formulas and processes. In a third class, students were working in small groups teaching their peers the method they used to solve a problem and discussing misconceptions that might have influenced someone to choose an incorrect strategy for solving the problem. Among the algebra classrooms, we also noted differences in the number of problems students were required to complete, but the problems were the same and represented the same standards. Perhaps the most notable finding was that the most experienced teacher and department head was teaching the students who needed the most support.

Pedagogy

Across all four high schools, although the teachers plan together to understand the standards and to determine how they will assess learning, instruction is neither rote nor scripted. Instead, teachers select and employ the instructional approaches they feel are most likely to engage their students and lead them to mastery. As one teacher at O'Farrell said:

> We have a lot of autonomy to work with the state standards, but teach them the way we feel best . . . There is a lot of flexibility to adapt curriculum to what's going on in the world, to address what's going on locally, nationally, globally and really bring that in.

Teachers at the four high schools shared a commitment to not just "addressing" or "covering" the standards, but to ensuring that all students achieved mastery of the standards. This shared commitment fueled collaboration as teachers sought to help each other lead all students to deep levels of understanding. Teachers recognized that no textbook or no one instructional strategy was going to work to lead every student to mastery. Teachers in all four schools believed that making these choices at the classroom level was very important. They are the leaders in their classrooms and know the students best, so having the autonomy to make meaningful instructional decisions, while also sharing the commitment to ensure each student's success propelled them to plan and improve instruction differently than if they followed a script produced by someone else.

Eastlake is a good example of teachers using different instructional methods in their classrooms. While some are experimenting with flipped classrooms, or using blended learning, others are using a more traditional direct-instruction approach with a gradual release of responsibility. Some teachers co-teach to improve inclusion and instruction for special education students and students learning English. After visiting several universities and colleges, Principal Martinez saw the importance of aligning Eastlake's instruction with college instruction that required more note taking at home and coming prepared to class with questions and participating in discussions. He also noted the rise in online classes and the importance of getting Eastlake students comfortable with the use of new technology. He wanted to ensure that Eastlake students could make a more seamless transition to college and university classrooms. But, Principal Martinez recognized that not every teacher is comfortable with technology or would be excited using some of the instructional methods used in college classrooms. So instead of insisting upon specific instructional strategies or particular uses of technology, he emphasizes the priority—student learning and readiness for college—and allows teachers some flexibility in how they approach the priority. However, for those who are ready to innovate, he provides multiple opportunities to learn from and observe exemplars. These teachers become models from whom other teachers learn. As one teacher said of her colleague who had flipped all of her classes, "I am in complete awe. I'm sitting here trying to figure out what I need to do. That is a goal of mine." The teachers shared ideas with one another and became a major source of each other's professional development. As a result, it was not uncommon to see the same strategies or lesson ideas across classrooms. Teachers were eager to share their best ideas and eager to borrow them from their colleagues.

Like at Eastlake, Revere teachers have been experimenting with technology and flipped classrooms, believing it helps students to take ownership of their learning and changes the teacher role to one of facilitator (which is more aligned with the new rigorous standards). To support implementation, Revere developed a space in their school called the Learning Common—an innovative learning environment designed to promote active learning, critical thinking, collaborative learning and knowledge building. It includes a lounge area, Smartboard area, genius bar staffed by students to support 1:1 iPad use, computer lab, reading nook and breakout rooms. But, Dr. Garcia and Revere teachers would like to go further and have competency drive the pace at which students move through the curriculum. They believe that greater attention to competency-based learning would increase the extent to which Revere students achieved deep understandings of important academic standards. O'Farrell is also beginning to use mastery to inform the pace of instruction as their math team seeks to implement standards-based grading.

Across all four schools, instructional innovations are often the suggestion of teachers or even students. For example, at Eastlake, the teacher who flipped all of her classes began with her AP Calculus class when her students asked if she would make videos they could watch at home, so they could use class time for questions, practice and application. Principals encourage faculty to bring ideas forward, provide the necessary professional development and support teachers as they pilot the innovations in their classrooms, all of which will be discussed in more detail in the next chapter.

In addition to focusing on standards and mastery, the educators in each school identify and pursue shared goals for instruction to build consistency for students and focus on the strategies they believe will support deeper learning. For example, O'Farrell is a National AVID demonstration school, so as a campus they are working on using inquiry and writing in every subject, as well as having students collaborate more during the learning process. They utilize certain practices including Socratic seminar, Cornell notes and binders to organize student work. At Revere High School, there are two focus areas for instruction being rolled out this coming year: text-based writing and Making Student Thinking Visible (MSTV). In order to have the focus areas influence everyday classroom instruction, directors, teacher leaders and administrators work as a team to make sure their efforts are aligned to support teachers in addressing the focus areas well. Best practices are shared during meetings and feedback is provided to staff as they work to implement new practices. For example,

MSTV is one of their newer initiatives and the teachers use their PLGs and planning groups to discuss their successes and challenges. As one teacher stated, "It's really about creating what's best for the students."

Most importantly, all the schools utilize a high demand, high support instructional approach (Ferguson, 2008). This approach emphasizes high expectations for student engagement in challenging academic and intellectual processes, while simultaneously providing high levels of support so that students are likely to progress toward success as they engage in stimulating educational classrooms. Characteristics of these classrooms include teachers who encourage students to ask questions, help students who are confused, and continually press students for both understanding and accuracy in their assignments. Teachers are more likely to have several ways of explaining things and also spend time getting to know about students' lives outside of school. Ferguson contends that students behave better and persist more when these two instructional conditions are present and the effect appears to be especially large for students of color. The combination of standards, expectations and support is what fuels the system in these four high schools.

Continuous Improvement

As well, the schools are invested in continuous improvement. Neither principals nor teachers at the four schools believed they were perfect and had all the answers. For example, at Pace, although they were intentional and purposeful about planning for instruction to ensure student learning, they realized far too much of their instruction was teacher directed. As a result, they have been moving towards more student-centered instruction, in particular, group assignments and collaborative learning experiences in classrooms. This shift in teaching required a change in delivery, not the standards or curriculum. They were fortunate to be participating in a grant to expand their early college high school program. Part of this work utilized the Common Instructional Framework (CIF), developed by Jobs for the Future, which identifies six powerful teaching and learning strategies to support students' college readiness (Jobs for the Future, 2012). They began with teachers already involved in the grant and then decided it would be useful for all teachers and moved to training the whole staff. One way that teachers operationalized the change was to improve upon their lesson plan format, building in ideas from the CIF to trigger thinking and intentionally selecting from among the six recommended instructional strategies (group work, questioning, writing to learn, classroom talk, scaffolding, and literacy groups).

Revere High School teachers are also focusing on student-centered learning. Every year, their goal is to dive deeper into implementation and improve. One Revere educator talked about the value of efforts to limit focus areas, by saying, "Focusing on three particular things, I think, has really calmed some people's nerves and allowed people to really dig deeper."

At Eastlake, Mr. Martinez developed a three-year plan when he opened the school. He noted, "My three-year plan was all about rigor, relevance, and relationships." The first two years, the school worked hard on building relationships, getting to know students personally, celebrating student accomplishments, and being clear about teacher expectations and their belief that students could meet them while simultaneously supporting students. Mr. Martinez explained, "The rigor couldn't come in unless we made it relevant." Now, with the help of specialized presenters, teachers were trained in different ways to improve rigor through relevance. His next steps are to offer more dual credit classes and become an AVID demonstration site, like O'Farrell.

These schools are not stagnant places, resting on their laurels. They are constantly striving to improve and meet the increasing expectations for more rigorous student learning.

Individualization, Intervention, and Enrichment

The schools are organized around providing a viable and guaranteed curriculum through collaboration and planning that focuses on priority standards, instructional strategies and assessment. In other words, educators plan so that students are more likely to learn concepts the first time they are taught. And, fewer students generally require intervention because the initial instruction (designed with the aid of strong teacher collaboration) is designed in a way to lead to student mastery. Nonetheless, in all four schools, classroom instruction is complemented with a robust support system and routines to further improve and extend learning. Support is not just encouragement, but rather is a system that complements classroom instruction and includes individualization, intervention, and enrichment to meet the needs of the student body.

Systematic Intervention

The educators in these schools want to ensure their students are prepared for postsecondary options, and they do what they can to help students deepen their understanding of the concepts and standards that are essential to student success. They do not simply present the content and hope the students get it, but rather they approach teaching and learning with a focus on mastery (Johnson, Perez, & Uline, 2012). Despite this focus, teachers understand that for a variety of reasons, some students may need additional support to meet the very high standards and expectations. Thus, timely and effective interventions are built into school structures and routines to ensure that all students access curricular rigor.

Each of the schools offers tutoring before and after school as well as during lunch or teacher free periods. Students, based on their commitments and schedules, need a variety of options and the teachers in these schools attempt to make this first line of defense easily accessible to students. The goal is to ensure student misconceptions are addressed and there are no gaps in learning that will hinder student progress. Students are encouraged and are able to see their classroom teachers, but they also know they can visit any teacher. Students talked about going to teachers they had relationships with that they thought might understand them better or know how they learn material better as well as seeing their classroom teachers.

Flexibility, adaptability, and a commitment to students are key elements of the intervention system. For example, at Pace, we observed a teacher as she ended a class period. She asked her students, how many would attend her afterschool tutorial session. Most students enthusiastically raised their hands; however, one student did not. The teacher expressed her eagerness to see her students at the tutorial session and quickly emphasized how the session was going to help them gain deeper understanding of the concepts they were studying. Then, she dismissed the students.

> As the students were leaving, she approached a boy who had not raised his hand. "Are you going to be at the tutorial this afternoon?" she asked.

He quickly responded, "No, I have to work."

The teacher sighed and said, "You are making such good progress in this class. I am so proud of how well you're doing. This tutorial could really help you succeed."

"But, I have to work. I can't miss work," the student responded with his head lowered.

"I understand," the teacher said, "but, I wish there was a way I could help you. Is there a way you can help me help you?"

After a pause, the student said, "Well, I could come in early tomorrow morning."

"Great!" the teacher responded. "I'll be here and together we will tackle this."

The teacher understood that no "one-size fits all" approach would work for all of her students. She was willing to work with her students and find solutions that worked for them. We saw evidence of this flexibility and adaptability at all four schools.

Many of the schools also offered Saturday school to accommodate student schedules and provide as many options as possible to help students master the material. Despite it being voluntary, many students attended to be able to work with their teachers. As one student said, "Teachers are doing this for us. We can at least show up." He was referring to a teacher who was tutoring for AP Calculus on Saturdays. Other teachers came in over spring break to administer mock AP testing to their students, provide practice and help students understand important concepts.

In addition to teachers going above and beyond for their students, the support structure is designed to be part of an overall system that promotes student success. For example, Eastlake accommodated their schedule and utilized resources to incorporate tutoring and extend learning to support the unique needs of their students. The school opens early (for a zero period) and closes late (for a ninth period) for tutoring. The school provides busing for those students who come early and leave late. As well, their academic calendar is a year-round hybrid with fall and spring intersessions and a one-month summer school in order for students to catch up or avoid falling behind. The principal believes "the earlier I can catch them, the better." But, Eastlake educators also make sure to leave no stone unturned and incorporate what they call "blitzes" into the school day if an important test for students is coming up and they know students need more practice with the material. Similarly, at Revere, during vacation weeks, teachers offer "ramp-up" classes in English and math to any student who needs more time in those subjects. These schools want to ensure intervention is timely, available and effective. Teachers use their planning time to analyze student data and work to plan targeted curricula for these interventions. More often than not, teachers are available for their own students, but they work as a team to ensure all students are getting what they need.

Tutoring is a common intervention that is widely available at these schools, but students also shared how teachers provided other solutions to poor grades. These solutions are student specific and are intended to support learning, not just getting points and credits to pass the class. They ranged from special projects to coming in and being interviewed by teachers to demonstrate their knowledge. These were not "easy passes" for students, they were intended to be different ways for students to access the curriculum and deepen their understanding to a level of satisfaction for the teachers.

Personalization and Special Programs

In addition to general support, educators at the four schools designed interventions and programs to respond to the needs of particular groups of students who continued to struggle despite intensive planning for instruction. For example, a few years back, Dr. García and his staff decided Revere needed a Freshman Academy to better support students with the transition from middle school to high school and also for those students who were new to the country. They wanted to ensure students understood the expectations for high school and felt creating a smaller learning environment would ensure students did not fall behind and stayed on track. It was a process that evolved organically among the staff based on their experiences with students. Despite the challenges they knew they were going to face to create a separate ninth grade academy, staff were ready to do what they felt was in the best interest of students. The freshman academy mission included five goals: provide a close knit, nurturing environment; foster the desire for life-long learning; enhance self-esteem; promote responsible citizenship; and develop the skills necessary for future success. The academy functions as a school within a school with its own space and teachers. Class sizes are deliberately reduced and teachers flexibly group students to personalize instruction and engage students in the learning process.

Revere educators did something similar for its English learner students who were coming to the high school from various countries, when they created a newcomer academy. They noticed that when these students were put in traditional classes, they came for a period of time, but were likely to drop out. To change this trajectory, students were put into a special academy to ramp up their English skills with an intensive curriculum— with the goal of moving them in about one year to the regular class-room. Students in the newcomer's academy are taught and supported by a cross-disciplinary, school-based team that includes bilingual educators, core academic content teachers, adjustment/guidance counselors and administrators to provide comprehensive educational services. Newcomer students are educated in a culturally and linguistically responsive teaching program, consistent with their level of English language proficiency and their academic needs. Instruction targets gaps in skills and knowledge that may result from limited or interrupted education. Since the inception of the Newcomers Academy in September 2013, many students have successfully made the transition to mainstream classes, where they have had the opportunity to graduate with other students who follow traditional learning pathways established for the high school.

One of the most important components of the support system at O'Farrell is "Home base," or what Principal Rainey calls "the secret sauce of O'Farrell." Rather than being a support system to remediate issues after they arise, it is both a proactive system to ensure "each student is known and loved by a teacher" as well as an on-demand system to provide a safe space to students to regroup if they are having issues in a class. Teachers start with a small group of students in freshman year and they have the same class/home base for all four high school years. It was not uncommon to hear students call their Home base teacher "Mom" or "Dad" and their peers, "my brother or sister." The home base class meets daily for the first 25 minutes of each school day. Students engage in team-building activities and have weekly grade checks on Friday. The teacher is fully responsible for the students including discipline, grades and communicating with home. In addition to starting the school day in Home base, students can return to Home base at any time during the day if they need support to get back on track to effectively participate in their classes. Students explained,

"Home base, that's like where your family is," or, "That's like your second actual family."

Similar to Home base, Revere High School worked into their master schedule time for Advisory. Revere students have an advisory teacher for all four high school years. In order to have 14–15 students in an advisory class, non-classroom teachers were assigned to lead an advisory. For example, the school library served as the classroom for several advisories for non-classroom teachers, including the librarian and the writing center coordinator. One student reported:

> Advisory is always that time where we can talk to our advisory teacher. She's kind of like our mom and she kind of reminds us of what we have to do. She's my confidence booster and I don't know—I just love advisory. Other than lunch, that's probably my favorite part of the day.

Another student said, "Advisory is just a moment to relax. It's just like a downtime. Sometimes we do circles, work on our portfolios or grade checks." Teachers and students see advisory as the perfect time to build and develop close relationships between teachers and students. The superintendent spoke about advisory and its purpose this way:

> Three days a week I get to meet with a special group of fourteen kids and I'm going to see them three days a week for the next four years and they're going to become mine and I'm going to become theirs and we're going to have a special bond.

For many students, advisory is a safe place to unwind and recharge, but teachers know what their students need and use the time effectively to make sure students are on track with their responsibilities.

Enrichment and Exposure

The support system is not solely about remediation, it also includes opportunities for enrichment and exposure the students might not experience on their own. The educators at all four schools think a lot about what will engage students and connect them to the school and their future. Many of their students arrive behind and they could spend all their time on catching students up, but they realize that these are young people who have goals and interests and educators take seriously their responsibility to help students explore their interests, find their passion and path after high school.

Enrichment looks different in every school yet the opportunities these schools give the students are valuable. Internships with local businesses, unique summer programs and dual enrollment in local colleges and certificate programs expand students' educational experiences. Counselors know the students interests and introduce them to opportunities they would otherwise not know about. One student at Pace was really excited to be a finalist for the Leadership Enterprise for a Diverse America Scholars program and attend the 7-week summer program at Princeton University. At Eastlake, students in different programs have the opportunity to travel to foreign countries, something that is typical of middle and higher income families but is not the norm for students who are often working to support their families. For example, the students who take computer science also take Chinese at the same time. As part of this dual class combination, the students traveled to Beijing. The students in the cosmetology program traveled to Italy. And, both the boys' and girls' soccer teams traveled to Spain. The school ensures that these trips are available to both higher and lower socioeconomic students. Students work to raise money themselves, but the school also works to get community sponsors for students who need extra help to ensure they do not miss out.

Even though O'Farrell is located in San Diego, a place where the ocean is twenty minutes away from the school, Dr. Dean, the super-intendent, realized many of their kids had never been to the beach. In order to expose his students to new opportunities, they took a group of students surfing. On another field trip, O'Farrell educators took a group of students snow skiing. Every year, the high school applies for grants to increase these types of opportunities. For example, all juniors are able to go on a college tour the summer before their senior year. They visit four to five colleges and spend the night on different college campuses to experience what it is like. That way, they are not surprised when they get to college. This experience has paid off; 100 percent of their graduating class applied to college.

Conclusion

A guiding principle in these four high schools (and the other NCUST award-winning high schools) is ensuring all students have access to the same curriculum and standards that are going to prepare them effectively for what comes after high school. The schools have clear visions of what success looks like, teachers are passionate about their subjects, and systems and routines support achievement of their goals. Educators work intentionally to plan instruction with their colleagues. Collaborative teams created safe spaces for teachers to learn, ask questions, try new instructional methods and support one another so all students reached mastery, not just some students. Intervention and enrichment were integral components to the system to ensure a floor was met, but also that there was no ceiling to what their students could accomplish. Educators are not satisfied with their students just learning low-level skills and getting by, they want their students to deeply understand topics and have opportunities to expand and connect their knowledge. Sometimes exposure is to fill gaps students may experience in their communities, but more often than not, educators are developing students' views about what is possible. Deeply embedded in the culture of these schools is the belief in the potential of each and every student.

Self-Assessment

1) What master schedule model have you selected?
   a) How is it aligned to your goals?
   b) Does it support achievement of your goals? What evidence do you have to support this?
2) How are teachers and time used in the master schedule?
   a) Are your more effective teachers teaching the students most in need?
   b) Are novice teachers teaching foundational courses and experienced teachers teaching advanced courses?
   c) How large are class sizes for foundational classes that students need to advance without remediation?

d) What percentage of classes are college prep?

e) Does the bell schedule maximize instructional time?

3) How student-centered is your master schedule?

a) How are students' interests reflected in the master schedule? List any examples.

b) Are students assigned to courses based on the need to fill seats or can students fully select their classes based on their goals and needs (e.g., advanced in one area, but not in another)?

c) Are extra classes built into the regular master schedule to help struggling students who need daily support to master rigorous coursework?

d) Are there extra classes available for students outside of the regular day for students who need more time to master rigorous coursework?

4) How do you ensure effective first instruction of what you want students to learn?

a) Do teachers who teach the same grade level/subject/course have common planning times? Who else attends these meetings? How often do teachers meet? How long does the common planning time last?

b) Typically, what happens during the common planning meetings? Are teachers regularly planning how they will teach priority standards?

c) As a result of collaborative planning, is instruction changing or are teachers using the same strategies, techniques, and lessons they used prior to planning?

d) Are English language learners provided access to core academic content using specifically designed instructional strategies?

5) How do you know if students have learned what you want them to learn?

a) In which courses do teachers administer common assessments that measure student attainment of priority standards for their course?

b) How often are common assessments administered?

c) What is done to help ensure that common assessments are valid and reliable measures of the priority standards that were taught?

d) After teachers administer common assessments, do they regularly meet to discuss and analyze the results? How do teachers address the numbers and percentages of students who mastered/did not master each priority standard assessed?

6) How do you respond when students do not achieve mastery?

a) Do collaborative teams review formative assessment results to learn specifically what students did not understand or what misconceptions might have prevented student mastery?

b) Are interventions structured to address the specific learning needs of students, including their misconceptions?

c) Do interventions occur in a timely manner, so that students receive help as soon as they need it (rather than waiting weeks or months to "fail" and then receive help)?

d) Who is available for intervention? Are they able to address student learning needs and misconceptions effectively?

7) How do you support students to extend their learning?

a) Is enrichment designed so all students can participate (in contrast to being available only to students who are academically successful)?

b) Is enrichment tailored to meet the needs and interests of students?

c) Does enrichment provide opportunities that are typically not available to students from low-income families?

d) Does enrichment provide opportunities for students to build long-standing, positive relationships with adults at school?

References

Bromberg, M., & Theokas, C. (2016). *Meandering towards graduation: Transcript outcomes of high school graduates*. Washington, DC: The Education Trust.

Ferguson, R. M. (2008). *Toward excellence with equity: An emerging vision for closing the achievement gap*. Cambridge, MA: Harvard Education Press.

Fullan, M. (2000). The three stories of education reform. Retrieved September 24, 2005, from *Change forces: Education in motion*, www.michaelfullan.ca/

Hanover Research. (2014). *Optimal scheduling for secondary school students*. Arlington, VA: Hanover Research.

Hattie, J. (2008). *Visible learning: A synthesis of over 800 meta-analyses relating to achievement*. New York: Routledge.

Jobs for the Future. (2012). Common instructional framework: Rubrics and support guides for teachers. Boston, MA: Jobs for the Future.

Johnson, J. F., Perez, L. G., & Uline, C. L. (2012). *Teaching practices from America's best urban schools: A guide for school and classroom leaders*. New York: Routledge.

Johnson, J. F., Uline, C. L., & Perez, L. G. (2017). *Leadership in America's best urban schools*. New York: Routledge.

Murray, L. (2011). *Diplomas matter: A field Guide for Educators*. New York: Jossey-Bass.

Oakes, J., & Guiton, G. (1995). Matchmaking: The dynamics of high school tracking decisions. *American Educational Research Journal, 32*(1), 3–33.

Theokas, C., & Saaris, R. (2013). *Finding America's missing AP and IB students*. Washington, DC: The Education Trust.

Vescio, V., Ross, D., & Adams, A. (2007). Review of research on the impact of professional learning communities on teaching practice and student learning. *Teaching and Teacher Education, 24*, 80–91.

Zepeda, S., & Mayers, R. S. (2006). An analysis of research on block scheduling. *Educational Research, 76*(1), 137–70.

Building Capacity

How do you get teachers to change their mindset? How do you get teachers to change how they deliver a lesson? How they plan for a lesson? We want them to feel supported. We want them to feel that we're in it with them, we're part of their team. We're part of their support staff. We're here to give them everything we have. We're here to give them suggestions. Yes, we're also administrators, so we have to discipline teachers when necessary, but they realize that that's not what we want. We're not there to get after them. We're there because we have the students' best interests in mind, and we know they do too.

—Pace, Dean of Instruction

Leaders in schools that achieved strong results for Latino students continuously sought to build the capacity of educators to meet the learning needs and capitalize upon the learning strengths of their Latino students. Specifically, leaders engaged faculty in identifying critical needs and opportunities for improving teaching and learning. Change was a team effort. Change was not isolated to a few classrooms. It was not a top-down mandate, but rather something that inspired the commitment of teachers, teacher leaders and administrators. These needs, identified by the team, became the problems of practice that educators and staff focused on throughout the year. Instead of pursuing a multitude of needs in a haphazard manner, these schools understood that students' needs are best addressed through a coordinated approach and by focusing narrowly on a few things each year. So, for example, an administrator at Revere said about their priorities:

So, I think we're going to continue those three big rocks for the next year or two to make sure we have consistency, and really, they become just part of the DNA or part of the way we do things before we layer something else on top of it.

Coordination was achieved by having professional development activities designed to emphasize the same core issues. These issues were then reinforced by administrators as they visited classrooms and observed teachers. And, teacher collaboration meetings were structured to ensure attention to the same core concepts, so teachers could better implement practices and help individual students meet challenging expectations. Through this powerful focus, even resistant staff began to acquire greater capacity to meet student needs (see Figure 5.1). Making change and asking teachers to do things differently can be very stressful, but each school established a culture of professional learning and continuous improvement as time and effort were dedicated to helping educators build efficacy and succeed with their students. The practice of continually reflecting upon and adjusting work based upon lessons learned helped make these schools very satisfying places for educators to work. They got to be masters of their practice. As one O'Farrell teacher said, "We try to be intentional. Let's try this. Let's do this. It's like a lab to hone our craft."

Just as capacity-building efforts were enhanced by a focus on a small number of priorities, they were also strengthened by a shared commitment to ensuring the success of every student. Educators understood *why* they were pursuing changes to what they taught, how they taught, or how their day was organized, so they were much more likely to approach professional development, collaboration, or observation and feedback as opportunities to help their students excel. They were less likely to perceive changes as administrative mandates (Johnson, Uline, & Perez, 2017).

Below, we share some of the issues the schools addressed and how they approached these changes as they moved along the path toward excellence and equity for all students. The critical needs varied because of local contexts, as did the tactics and models employed to improve, but at the heart of most of the improvements was a focus on building consistency in instruction and ensuring students were challenged, engaged and benefitting from the work associated with learning challenging standards. Educators in all four schools were working in the broader social/political/educational context associated with the transition to more

Figure 5.1 Steps Toward Capacity Building

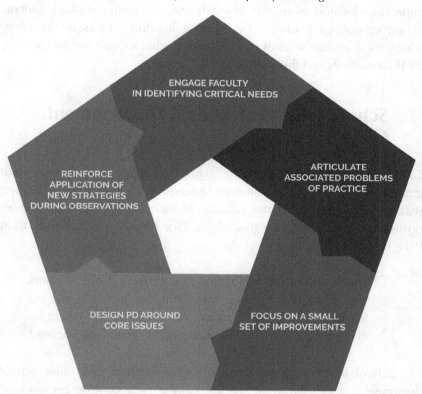

rigorous standards and they realized if their Latino students were going to compete with other students in the ever-changing knowledge economy, their students needed to be able to apply information, not just sit and get it from teachers, so they endeavored to engage more student-centered strategies.

Moreover, educators recognized that their efforts to improve instruction for one group of students often benefitted all students, which helped reinforce shared goals and priorities. For example, the focus on building students' academic vocabulary was helpful to their Latino English learner students, but it also supported other students in developing an extensive academic vocabulary. Similarly, when teachers endeavored to implement instructional strategies typically used with gifted and talented students, they found that those strategies were often useful for engaging students who were still struggling to build foundational skills. By focusing on the instructional needs of specific groups of students who needed to improve, educators were able to maximize the likelihood of all students achieving college readiness by bringing important ideas to the table. Educators at all four schools had a vision of what success would look like for their students and this was their guiding star.

School-wide Professional Development Goals

Each principal, whether building a new school from an initial ninth grade cohort or coming into an existing school with an established history, was focused on building the capacity of their staff to meet the goal of postsecondary readiness for all students. One of the assistant principals at Pace described it this way:

> The key to our kids' success in education is our teachers. You must have the best instruction, all the time. All our teachers want is to be supported. That's all they want, so that's our job. We provide that support so students succeed.

School leaders, in collaboration with teachers and other school personnel, established what we are calling "school-wide professional development goals" that articulated specific ways in which teaching and learning should improve. As mentioned at the beginning of this chapter, there were not many professional development goals. The goals did not change frequently. And, perhaps most importantly, the goals were intended to promote practices that would lead more students to achieve readiness for success in postsecondary settings.

Leaders felt responsible for developing systems that would provide abundant, high-quality support that helped educators improve teaching and learning in specific ways. First, however, staff needed to understand both what needed to change and why. Mrs. Longoria, at Pace, joked that she met with teachers so often and talked about the needs of the students so much, that teachers would run from her. However, her actions were intentional. She wanted to be clear about what she expected to see in classrooms and she wanted teachers to understand why the changes would make a difference for Pace students. Also, she wanted teachers to understand how she and other Pace leaders would support them with professional development and training, so they would successfully make the desired changes. The only way she could achieve this clarity was by being in teachers' classrooms and talking with them about instruction. When asked why Pace was so successful, one teacher said, "We had something mapped out for us and Mrs. Longoria knew how to adhere to it, guide us and support us."

At Pace and the other three high schools, teachers did not see their school-wide professional development goals as administrative mandates. Instead, they perceived that the goals were co-created by teachers and administrators. They recognized and appreciated the influence of their leaders; however, the goals belonged to the entire professional team.

Mrs. Longoria also noted the importance of helping teachers see the outcome toward which they were working. By providing teachers opportunities to see desired teaching practices implemented well, teachers gained a deeper understanding of what they were being asked to improve about their teaching. Thus, Mrs. Longoria and her leadership team provided many opportunities for teachers to observe each other.

O'Farrell leaders also provided opportunities for teachers to showcase what they were doing in their classroom for other teachers. Outside the teachers' mailboxes is a board with a Pineapple Chart (Gonzales & Barnes, 2015) where teachers can post things they are doing in their classroom other teachers might like to know about and observe. This often inspires other teachers and helps build the professional culture of educators. Richard Elmore once argued that education does not have a practice (Elmore, 1996). To improve teaching at scale, he believed the field had to develop a set of protocols, conventions, norms, common language and a set of ideas about how practices look when implemented. Each of these schools was attempting to do so by opening up classrooms for discussion and learning. A teacher at O'Farrell noted:

> It is really nice that we are supported in how we grow.
> We can see it and not just talk about it in our meetings.
> To visually see what is happening in other classrooms
> helps me understand how it works.

While Pace leaders wanted teachers to see good examples, Mrs. Longoria cautioned that teachers needed to take on manageable chunks they could tackle. The end goal can seem so unattainable that teachers may not perceive that the dramatic changes necessary are worth the effort required. Mrs. Longoria explained, "We had to show them it was possible."

Ultimately, capacity building at the four schools was intentional and systematic. There were intentional efforts to build the capacity of teachers and other school personnel to prepare students for postsecondary success. This is substantially different from the random acts of professional development that occur in some schools. As well, it is different from the long teacher observation checklists used in many school districts.

Teacher collaboration, professional development, and observation, feedback, and support strategies were tightly aligned into systems that help teachers perceive that both administrators and other teachers wanted them to succeed. The strategies were interwoven in ways that helped teachers meet school-wide professional development goals. The concepts and skills teachers learned in professional development sessions were often the focus of planning in teacher collaboration meetings. School leaders often noted progress related to the same concepts and skills when they observed classrooms and provided feedback and support to teachers. The focus on a limited number of school-wide professional development goals facilitated this coherence.

While it is common for school leaders to expect teachers to improve teaching and learning, it is uncommon to see school leaders demonstrating a high level of personal responsibility for helping teachers successfully improve teaching and learning, in accordance with the school-wide professional development goals. However, in the four schools studied, leaders worked relentlessly to help teachers understand what was expected, understand why the changes would benefit students and receive access to abundant high-quality assistance through outside experts and from peers, through traditional professional development sessions and through in-classroom support and with many opportunities to try, receive constructive feedback, and try again. Leaders made it their responsibility to find multiple ways to help teachers understand, learn and improve their professional practice in ways that would benefit the students they served.

At each of the four schools, the school-wide professional development goals evolved over time. However, they were always focused on a small number of teaching practices that had proven effective helping students master challenging academic standards. For example, at both Pace and Revere, Mrs. Longoria and Dr. Garcia placed an initial focus on moving toward student-centered instruction. Later, Pace refined their focus with an emphasis on the Common Instructional Framework. Similarly, Revere focused more specifically on Making Student Thinking Visible. Educators at Eastlake chose the Fundamental Five Program, while O'Farrell committed to developing AVID strategies.

Importantly, the goal was not simply to have professional development sessions. Leaders rejected traditional "drive-by" professional development. As an Eastlake administrator explained, "Do it one time and how do you expect teachers to learn. You have to come back to it and each time get a deeper understanding so that it can become old-hat." Similarly, the goal was not to observe teachers and force them to change their practice. Instead, the goal was to build the capacity of school personnel to implement specific instructional practices that had a high likelihood of promoting better learning results for all students.

Professional Development Principles and Methods

Each school had some time in their regular schedule dedicated to professional development. Who conducted it and when and how long it occurred varied based on resources, needs and also the school's stage of implementation. However, we noticed the following principles across all four schools:

- School personnel were thoughtful about who could best build their capacity to achieve the school-wide professional development goals. All schools used consultants and outside experts as needed. For example, Mrs. Longoria said, "We had Martha Morales help us. I do a lot of research on what works in other districts who are achieving success . . . So, she has this program that's supposed to be fantastic. I put money aside and I sent all of the teachers to it." Also, the schools utilized the expertise of teachers and administrators within their buildings. In some cases, school personnel did not have the necessary expertise, so the leaders identified individuals with a strong interest in the professional development approach who would receive intensive training and support. As those individuals developed expertise, they assumed responsibility for providing training and support to their colleagues. For example, a teacher at Revere said, "The best part of professional development is usually once we have these outside trainings, a group of teachers become our teacher leaders. Making Student Thinking Visible was a course from an outside provider. But, we now have a cohort of teachers who are the MSTV coaches/experts. That's what we are calling them."

- Professional development is ongoing. Educators at these schools are focused on continuously improving. For example, even though O'Farrell has been recognized as a National AVID Demonstration School, teachers still receive professional development on AVID teaching strategies.

- Leadership participated in all trainings and took responsibility for maintaining the focus. For example, Dr. Garcia pointed out, "it's not just designing it and putting it out there and saying do it; you have to be willing, you have to embed with teachers, with the teaching force to make sure it succeeds."

- Teachers perceived professional development activities as highly relevant to their everyday work in classrooms. Teacher's perception of relevance was essential for initial buy-in and continued growth. One teacher at O'Farrell described professional development this way, "Every year we have a PD theme and it is always targeted to help support students and teachers in the classroom. This year we did critical reading, in past years we did other AVID strategies, and then years ago we did sheltered English immersion training to help ELL students. Every year, it is something we can use in the classroom."

- New innovations are researched, piloted with small groups and expanded when resources are in place and bugs are worked out.

- Teacher use their collaborative planning structures (e.g., PLCs) to plan how they will implement what they learned in professional development. Administrators and other leaders will reinforce concepts and skills learned through professional development as they observe classrooms and provide feedback. The synergy between professional development, teacher collaboration, and classroom observations and feedback increases the likelihood that everyday instructional practices improve.

These principles are illustrated in the professional development journey of each of the four schools. The journeys described below illustrate how professional development did not jump from one topic to the next randomly. Instead, educators deliberately endeavored to build their capacity in ways that responded to their current strengths and needs, while aiming toward a quality and consistency of teaching and learning across classrooms that would ensure the success of all students at their schools.

Pace Early College High School

As described previously, Pace educators embraced a school-wide professional development goal designed to build the capacity of teachers to utilize a student-centered approach to teaching, in contrast to a teacher-directed approach. Many Pace teachers had graduated from Pace or other Brownsville schools and had been teaching at Pace for many years. Many Pace teachers had learned to use lectures as their primary instructional tool. Mrs. Longoria helped teachers recognize that they were more likely to help Pace students achieve college readiness if they shifted to instructional strategies that engaged and responded to the needs of the students they served.

Pace benefitted from a Texas Title I Priority Schools grant in the first few years of their transformation. Pace leaders used the grant resources to purchase equipment that could be used to increase student engagement in learning (e.g., LCD projectors and Mobi pads). These tools required training and support. Leaders focused the training on how teachers could use the resources to advance student engagement.

The next year, Pace leaders broadened the focus to help teachers learn how to build collaborative learning activities and use higher order thinking skills questions during instruction. This training provided Pace teachers with more strategies for increasing the engagement of students in discussions of challenging academic content.

As Pace continued its journey, they also chose to be part of an Investing in Innovation grant (I3), which was an early college high school expansion program. The training for the early college high school teachers was focused on using the Common Instructional Framework, which is built on the premise that when you let students take charge of their learning, they succeed. This approach extended the professional development goals Pace educators had previously established and supported a deeper understanding of how to effectively plan lessons that supported group work, problem solving and writing. A few teachers were trained and received coaching to implement the practices in their classrooms. Now, the training has expanded to the whole staff and Pace uses their expert teachers as models for other teachers.

This past year, educators at Pace determined that they still need to improve their instruction in ways that will better ensure the success of their English language learners. A number of teachers were trained in a program researched by Mrs. Longoria to help improve the reading comprehension of English learners. The teachers who received the training initially are now the leaders for other teachers.

Eastlake High School

At Eastlake, they chose the Fundamental Five model, developed by Sean Cain, as a vehicle to improve the quality of instruction across the campus. Like the Common Instructional Framework utilized at Pace, the Fundamental Five identifies critical practices that are at the heart of highly effective instruction, such as frequent small group purposeful talk and critical writing. Eastlake leaders asked teachers to make a conscious commitment to improving their teaching practice. After going through the training, teachers described looking at their instructional delivery differently, from how their classrooms were arranged to making sure to adjust their instruction across the course of a lesson based on student feedback. Eastlake has used the Fundamental Five model for a number of years. To support implementation, the assistant principals conduct walkthroughs and provide feedback specific to the five elements. Rubrics help teachers identify strengths and weaknesses and administrators focus on helping staff improve in those areas. Eastlake leaders noted it can be challenging for teachers to receive low scores because they care so much, but the honest feedback provides administrators with an opportunity to talk specifically about the practice being observed and the support they can provide to help teachers succeed. As well, Eastlake leaders reinforce that instructional improvement is a team effort and process, not a simple checklist. Teaching in ways that lead all students to postsecondary readiness takes a lot of time and planning.

Administrators at Eastlake were supported in providing good feedback to teachers. The district offered cognitive coaching training to administrators to learn about how to ask questions to elicit responses from teachers, based on an analysis of their practice. Administrators did not want to present a preconceived notion of what "correct" instruction looked like, but rather have teachers reflect on the choices they were making and what was leading to student learning. Administrators felt this was helping teachers feel free to try new things and expand their capacity rather having them follow a formula.

The O'Farrell High School

O'Farrell also chose a model to help them focus and continue to improve their work as they grew as a school; Advancing Via Individual Determination (AVID). Currently, the school is a National AVID Demonstration Site, but nonetheless they are constantly trying to improve their implementation of AVID strategies to benefit students. All teachers have been trained in AVID strategies and methodologies; some have received more in-depth training in their particular subject area, while others have been more globally trained. This past year, to deepen their practice, as a staff they focused on critical reading and how all teachers could implement strategies in their classrooms to improve student skills. The yearlong focus on critical reading includes professional development around the topic on the first Wednesday of the month.

O'Farrell teachers described professional development in previous years that focused on other AVID strategies, but they also received training in sheltered English immersion, their instructional model for their English learner population. Also, they received training on incorporating social emotional development into their lessons.

Revere High School

During Dr. Garcia's first year of leadership at Revere, the focus of professional development was supporting teachers as they endeavored to manage and engage students during 80-minute block periods. The school transitioned to this new schedule, so students might better meet rigorous student learning goals. Each year since then, Revere leaders and teachers have worked to increase their skills related to creating student-centered learning environments, where both teachers and students could take ownership for their learning. They have focused on implementation of their advisory period, text-based writing and more recently Making Student Thinking Visible (MSTV). Each year, Revere educators delve deeper into the practices, learning from and supporting one another.

The pursuit of these strategies is enhanced by frequent observations from Revere administrators. As one administrator said:

> We try to prod, poke, and pry people into those strategies, making sure that when we meet for their formative meetings we ask them, "So what kind of strategies have you used to bring Text-Based Writing to your classroom? Or, which of the 24 operating principles of MSTV have you found to be most effective? What have you done in your Advisory to build relationships? How are the gatherings going?" So, because all of us are focusing on the same few things, hope-fully we have brought about consistency.

Professional development at Revere has evolved as they have developed increased clarity and precision around their school goals and what they need to do as a staff to reach their goals. By regularly observing classrooms with a focus on the implementation of the practices that were the focus of professional development, Revere leaders realized that they had teacher experts who could teach the professional development strategies as well as anyone. One teacher described her experience with professional development over 20 years at Revere by saying:

> When I first started working here in 1996, they would bring in a lot of outside people to tell us stuff, [and call it 'professional development']. Now teachers run almost all of our directors' meetings. So, for example, I'm taking one on writing that's being taught by two of my colleagues, and it's probably the best director's meeting I have ever done in my life. It goes by quickly and I can't wait for it to happen.

The goal of professional development is to build capacity at the school level, so Revere uses a train-the-trainer model. Dr. Garcia shared that they partner with outside providers as there are many experts out there, they wish to learn from, but at the outset of all these relationships he lets them know:

We want to buy into your professional development, but you need to work with a handful of teachers who are going to become the school experts in this professional development. We want to commit them to a couple of extra days to train with you and they are going to guide their colleagues as we make this implementation change.

In this way, the professional development becomes ongoing and embedded into the work of teachers. The teachers who received the extra training facilitate other professional development sessions at the school over the year or are available to answer questions. They also do observations of colleagues and provide feedback or colleagues come and observe them in their classrooms. This model allows teachers opportunity to practice; reflect on what worked, what did not and why; and work together to support each other as they continue to improve.

In order to carry out this shift, Revere's organizational structure was redesigned and reinforced with different procedures to support teacher leadership. The campus has 12 student-centered learning committees that are pursuing new knowledge and understanding they can bring back to their colleagues. Each committee decides upon goals and action steps and creates a plan for the year. There is a school redesign and innovation committee that oversees these committees to monitor and track progress and to ensure alignment and communication. The next step Revere would like to take is to develop a competency-based grading system to support the student-centered learning environment they have been creating the last several years. A small group of teachers has been working on this for about a year. Dr. Garcia knows this shift is, ". . . going to take a long time to accomplish." So, he is happy a small group of teachers are already working on it and can help lead the transition when they are ready.

Observation, Feedback, and Support

As indicated in the discussion of professional development principles and methods, professional development activities were enhanced both by teacher collaboration and by regular cycles of classroom observation, feedback, and support. It is difficult to separate these elements because they combine to create a system intended to build the capacity of school personnel to help all students succeed academically. In Chapter Four, we described the nature of teacher collaboration in the four schools. In this section, we describe the nature of classroom observation, feedback and support.

It is important to note that building the capacity of teachers to help all students succeed was one of the primary purposes of classroom observations, feedback and support at the four schools studied. Often, in more typical schools, observation and feedback has a primary purpose of evaluating teacher performance. So, it is not surprising that many teachers in typical schools dread having administrators (or even colleagues) observe their classrooms. In contrast, at the four schools studied, observation and feedback sessions were specifically designed to help teachers succeed. Focus was on continuous improvement, based on the belief that caring professional educators wanted to find ways to continuously improve their service to students. As well, the focus on continuous improvement was based on the belief that strong administrators and teacher leaders should strive to provide a quality of support that makes it easier for teachers to continuously improve their craft.

Observation, Feedback, and Support Principles

Although observation, feedback and support differed across the four schools, the following principles were consistently applied:

- School leaders and administrators are frequently in classrooms observing and providing constructive feedback related to the efficacy of instruction. Educators at all of the schools stressed that the visibility of leaders was important to the functioning of the school and ultimately meeting their goals. For example, Mr. Rainey at O'Farrell reported:

  > I walk into classrooms all the time. Every day, I step into a classroom, even if it's just taking the temperature. I look around constantly. I have formal walk-through observations that I do and informal evaluation observations, but I am just out there constantly.

  Frequent observations and feedback helped increase the likelihood that the concepts and skills learned in professional development sessions were implemented and practiced in classrooms. To maximize the frequency, principals coordinated their observation efforts, along with assistant principals, department chairs and instructional coaches.

- Clarity was a critical attribute of observation and feedback efforts in the four schools. Like professional development, observation and feedback were not haphazard or random. Teachers clearly understood what observers expected to see, related to their school-wide professional development goals. Administrators focused their feedback in ways that clearly aligned to the concepts and skills that were the focus of professional development. One teacher at Eastlake told us:

> They've also made it very clear as to what they want to see. We have been told, "We want to see this and this in your room. We're going to look for this." And so, it's not a surprise. "What? You wanted me to do this?" No, they've told you exactly. And then, your department leaders will go back and let the department know, so it's not a surprise. They let us know what's expected of us.

- Observations and feedback are intended to promote improved implementation. They are not intended to punish teachers. At struggling schools, we find that teachers are much less receptive to classroom observations because there is a clear lack of trust. Teachers suspect that administrators observe their classrooms with the primary intent of finding fault. In contrast, at the four schools studied, both teachers and administrators emphasized that observations were intended to support teachers. As one administrator at Eastlake said:

> If we have to get to the point where we're documenting teachers or maybe a non-renew, we inform our principal, first and foremost, but we try to intervene, so it doesn't get to that point because our job is to coach a teacher, to help them strengthen their skills and make them better educators and not necessarily to fire them.

Teachers reported that they looked forward to the visits because they appreciated the objective feedback. For example, an Eastlake teacher explained:

> I like the walkthroughs because if I'm not doing something right, or if I can do it better, I'd like to get that feedback. As we get our results, I like to know how I'm doing. I might be thinking that I'm not doing so good, but when I see [the feedback], it's like 'Oh my God, I'm doing really well.' So, it feels good that they're giving you that feedback.

- Responsibility for conducting observations was shared across administrators and teacher leaders; however, there was a high level of consistency across observers. Leadership teams often conducted walkthroughs as a group to ensure they were aligned and calibrated and were giving consistent feedback to teachers. Some of the questions leaders considered during observations included:

  - Does the lesson lead students to the level of rigor demanded by the targeted standard?
  - Which students are providing clear evidence that they understand what the teacher is teaching? Which students are not?
  - Which students are demonstrating a high level of engagement in the lesson? Which students are not?
  - Are there specific groups of students who are not demonstrating evidence of mastery?
  - What could the teacher do to increase the likelihood that more students demonstrate mastery?
  - What is the tone of the classroom and the nature of relationships among students and teachers?

- Feedback and support frequently accompanied or followed observations. Teachers were not left to wonder what observers saw or thought about their teaching. Administrators and teacher leaders provided prompt (sometimes immediate) feedback. In some cases, the feedback was a short note emphasizing that the teacher demonstrated a specific professional development practice well. In other cases, the feedback was a more extensive conversation. Often leaders asked questions to better understand what the teacher was attempting to accomplish or why the teacher used a particular approach. For example, O'Farrell's principal, Mr. Rainey explained:

I have a conversation with the teacher like, "What was that thing you were doing. That was different or interesting or whatever." I have them explain it and hear their thinking. I try not to assume. Because when you walk into a classroom, it's a tiny snapshot. They're professionals. Give them the benefit of the doubt.

Teachers valued the time leaders spent in classrooms because of the constructive feedback and support they received. Teachers perceived that the feedback and support 1) was sincerely intended to support them and 2) consistently helped them get their students to master important concepts and skills. Leaders thoughtfully considered what support might help a teacher achieve better learning outcomes for her students.

Sometimes, a teacher might have just needed a conversation about what the leader observed and the chance to reflect upon the lesson with someone who cared. Sometimes, a teacher might have needed additional support with an instructional coach who would go into the classroom, model a teaching strategy and co-teach with the teacher. At other times, a teacher might have needed an opportunity to go watch an excellent teacher demonstrate a specific practice. Leaders were sensitive to the type of feedback and support teachers were most likely to need, given their personality, strengths, learning styles, and needs.

Culture of Learning

The efforts to build capacity in the four schools resulted in a culture of learning for both students and adults (see Figure 5.2). Educators (including teachers, administrators and support staff) took pride in their ongoing efforts to learn and improve their craft. Educators did not act as if perfection was required or even possible. Even when they were performing well and achieving remarkable results, educators still were thirsty to learn and improve outcomes for students.

Leaders established a culture that respected the varying strengths and needs of each individual educator. Educators were not expected to learn at the same rate or demonstrate proficiency on the same skills at the same moment. Leaders inspired commitment and effort, nurtured growth and improvement and acknowledged and celebrated contributions that were leading to better learning results for students.

Figure 5.2 Culture of Learning Fundamentals

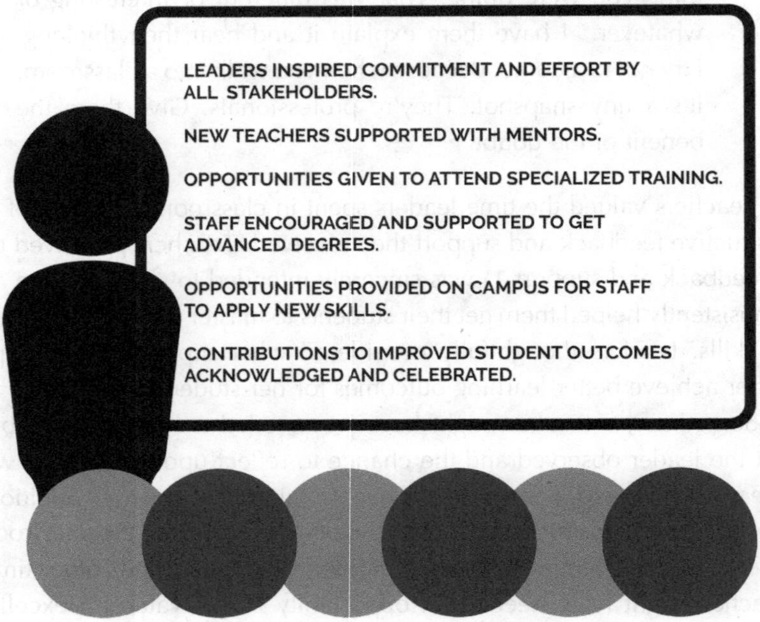

LEADERS INSPIRED COMMITMENT AND EFFORT BY ALL STAKEHOLDERS.

NEW TEACHERS SUPPORTED WITH MENTORS.

OPPORTUNITIES GIVEN TO ATTEND SPECIALIZED TRAINING.

STAFF ENCOURAGED AND SUPPORTED TO GET ADVANCED DEGREES.

OPPORTUNITIES PROVIDED ON CAMPUS FOR STAFF TO APPLY NEW SKILLS.

CONTRIBUTIONS TO IMPROVED STUDENT OUTCOMES ACKNOWLEDGED AND CELEBRATED.

All four schools supported new teachers with some type of mentor relationship, whether with an experienced teacher in their department or with an instructional coach or assistant principal who provided specialized training. Experienced teachers and administrators were encouraged and supported to get masters' and doctoral degrees. While pursuing their studies, opportunities were provided on campus for educators to learn and apply new skills. For example, at Eastlake, aspiring administrators were given the chance to coordinate intersessions, the tutorial program and department meetings; teachers were given the opportunity to become certified to teach dual-credit courses.

As well, teachers were given opportunities to attend specialized trainings. For example, teachers at both Eastlake and O'Farrell have attended AVID, Advanced Placement and the National Math and Science Institute Summer Trainings to grow their skills. One teacher at O'Farrell reflected:

> As teachers we can ask [to go to trainings], as department chairs, they can ask for a department to be trained. I know last Wednesday our history department was out learning the

new history standards. Our science department has gone out this year and learned the new Next Generation Science (NGSS) standards. This summer, we have a bunch of teachers going to the AVID Summer Institutes. So, there are professional development opportunities available if teachers are proactive and asking, but then we also have in-house professional development like the year-long training and going to various classrooms and that type of stuff.

So, while there is a sincere respect for the learning needs of individual educators, it is important to note that the culture of learning is fundamentally a team culture at all four schools. There is a team commitment to learning and growing in ways that will improve outcomes for all the students served. The academic coach at O'Farrell described the culture of learning in this way:

> There's this openness to fine tune and improve and so, there's nothing about O'Farrell that is stagnant. But it's not changing just to be trendy. You have to argue your plan, your proposal, your idea and not just to someone above you. You have to convince your peers. There's a peer leadership model here that is very strong.

Conclusion

We do a lot of professional development here at the high school. We want to make sure that our teachers feel confident that they have the resources and materials to be able to give the students an effective education. That's where we may be different. A school district, in my view, is built for staff and bureaucracy. Ours is built for kids and although districts want to be—and in our heart, I believe, they want to be for kids, it just innately is different because the bureaucracy and the staff take over. Whether it be unions, whether it be groups or individuals. Here, I always try to focus upon the kids. So, if the teachers want something, even professional development, their opening sentence has to be about how is it going to affect kids.

So, it's almost become a joke here because I'll start off with that first sentence and then move into what they want.
—O'Farrell Superintendent, Dr. Dean

Urban high schools are complex places and more commonly you find educators isolated in their silos pursuing their subject matter and methods of teaching. Teachers from different departments often do not know each other and administrators are rarely in classrooms. There is an implicit question that if you have not taught biology or whatever specialized course a high school teacher teaches, how in the world could you understand what the teacher was doing and provide meaningful feedback about their instruction? In these four high schools, a common goal and vision directed the actions of the whole staff and professional development, observations and evaluations were used to build capacity to help staff reach the school goals. These were important elements of the school design and were used strategically and intentionally. Educators in these schools were not dreading the monthly Wednesday meeting or when an administrator came into their classroom. Instead, it was seen as time to reflect, get feedback, and improve their professional practice. They benefitted from external expertise, but also looked at their colleagues as possible sources of inspiration, information and ideas. And, as the schools built their internal capacity, they created their own cycles of continuous improvement further developing their focus areas and goals. Building this culture of learning and the capacity of educators occurred over time and continues to evolve at these four schools, but they believe the hard work is worth the effort to improve the quality of learning for students.

Self-Assessment

1) What evidence suggests that there is a coordinated, sustained effort to build the capacity of educators to ensure the success of all students (including Latino students)?

2) To what extent are capacity-building efforts focused on a small set of priorities? To what extent are efforts directed toward a wide array of professional development initiatives?

3) Have educators at your school developed specific school-wide professional development goals?

a) To what extent do educators have a common understanding of what each goal means and what quality implementation looks like?

b) To what extent do educators share a common understanding of why each professional development goal is important to the academic success of students?

c) To what extent do educators perceive ownership in establishing and pursuing the professional development goals?

4) In what ways do teacher collaboration activities (e.g., PLC meetings) contribute to capacity building efforts and the pursuit of your school-wide professional development goals?

5) In what ways do professional development activities contribute to capacity building efforts and the pursuit of your school-wide professional development goals?

a) To what extent do professional development activities increase the likelihood that teachers will improve their regular implementation of practices associated with the school-wide professional development goals?

b) To what extent do school leaders engage teachers from the school in providing professional development for colleagues? How are decisions made about who can best provide the professional development needed?

c) To what extent do administrators and teacher leaders actively engage in the professional development activities in which teachers are expected to participate?

d) To what extent do teachers perceive professional development activities as relevant to their everyday work in classrooms?

6) In what ways do classroom observations, feedback, and support contribute to capacity building efforts and the pursuit of your school-wide professional development goals?

a) To what extent do classroom observations, feedback and support increase the likelihood that teachers will improve their implementation of practices associated with the school-wide professional development goals?

b) How frequently are teachers likely to be observed by administrators? By peers? How frequently are they likely to receive feedback related to observations?

c) To what extent is there shared clarity about what observers are looking to find when they visit classrooms?

d) To what extent do teachers perceive that observations and feedback are intended to support their efforts and help them succeed? To what extent do teachers perceive that observations are intended to "catch" them doing something wrong and punish them?

e) To what extent is there a high level of consistency among the various individuals who observe teachers at the school?

f) To what extent do teachers feel supported as a result of observations and feedback?

References

Elmore, R. (1996). Getting to scale with good educational practice. *Harvard Educational Review*, 66(1), 1–26.

Gonzalez, J., and Barnes, M. D. (2015). *Hacking education: 10 quick fixes for every school*. Cleveland, OH: Times 10 Publications.

Johnson, J. F., Uline, C. L., & Perez, L. G. (2017). *Leadership in America's best urban schools*. New York: Routledge.

6

Strengthening Teaching and Learning Through the Use of Data

A lot of the decisions that we make for the students, as far as activities and interventions that we have in place for them, are based on the data that we get from exams, both informal and formal ones. But in order for us to really have an impact, it's the relationships that we establish with the students first and foremost before we can actually get them to understand the data. 'This is what happened on this exam but I believe in you. I know that you can do a lot better. These are the next steps we're going take.' At that point, the student is like, 'Okay, I know I messed up. I know that I can do better. Help me.' And they know that we're there for them.

—A Revere educator

Across the country, urban high schools struggle with how best to meet the learning needs of the students they serve. Many school administrators and teachers, impelled by their sense of urgency, quickly turn to the next, new intervention program, textbook, or instructional strategy in hopes that it will provide the support students need. In contrast, the educators in these four urban high schools employed rigorous systems for using data to identify strategies that fit the particular needs of the students served. We found that educators collected, monitored and acted upon a wide array of data (e.g., attendance data, discipline, common formative assessment data, benchmark or quarterly assessments, graduation rates, college acceptance rates, college matriculation rates) in ways that helped ensure that Latino students were likely to succeed. That said, when we asked the various stakeholders during our interviews and focus groups, what they believed contributed to their Latino students' success, data was never the first thing on educators' lists.

This was particularly interesting as more often than not we were sitting in a room that had data posted all over the walls. At Pace, for example, we were sitting in their so-called "war room" that had individual student data color-coded by current status on benchmark assessments and school-wide ACT/SAT scores, AP enrollment and pass rates, Texas Success Initiative assessment (TSI) outcomes and attendance. So, when we asked the degree to which they used data to inform decisions, the most common reaction was that data was essential to understand their students' needs. For example, the academic coach at O'Farrell said, "For me, [data are] everything, to the point where I think sometimes teachers run away from me when they see me coming at them with Excel sheets." Pace principal Rose Longoria shared a similar response. "We are so data-driven. That is like the biggest, biggest, biggest thing." Ultimately, for these schools, the combination of data sources provided a new window into their students' success. As Ms. Longoria concluded, "You have got to know each kid."

The original effective schools research and our own research on high-performing urban schools supports that a clear assessment of mastery is essential to students' success (Chenoweth & Theokas, 2011; Edmonds, 1979; Johnson, Uline, & Perez, 2017). If educators are not focused on what they want their students to learn and if they do not have a way of measuring it, there are significant limitations to what they can accomplish. Large groups of students could be falling through the cracks with no one knowing or the rigor of instruction might not match the standard reducing students' opportunity to learn. Although educators in these four schools were not immediately pointing to data as a reason for their success, a clear assessment of mastery was built into these schools' operations. For them, data were inexorably integrated into the educational system, as were their beliefs about students. You cannot pull them apart. They believed their students were capable of learning just about anything they were capable of teaching them and the wise use of data was a part of the process to help them know if students were mastering the academic content and how to advance their mastery.

How Schools Organize and Prioritize the Use Data

An unprecedented amount of data is available to educators, and it is packaged in more efficient ways than ever before. All four of the schools have some type of student information system (e.g., Illuminate, Power School, Eduphoria, etc.) that collects, aggregates and displays data for both students and staff to use to make decisions. That said there are multiple types of data (e.g., demographic, enrollment, attendance, engagement, discipline, achievement, on-track indicators, etc.) and multiple ways to use data (e.g., data to inform instruction or data for accountability purposes). As well, data can be formal or informal, objective (e.g., test results), or subjective (e.g., survey results), formative, or summative, which has implications for its use and data are available at different levels of analysis for insights (e.g., individual, classroom, student group, etc.).

This complexity points to the fact that data-driven educational decision-making is far more than a data system. Data needs to be transformed into usable information. Educators in these schools are not just asking, "Who passed?" They are trying to understand, "What do the students know and not know?" And, "What are we going to do about it." These schools have created a culture that incorporates a set of expectations and practices around the ongoing examination of student data to ascertain the effectiveness of educational activities and subsequently to refine programs and practices to improve outcomes for students.

One of the directors at Revere described the culture shift that occurred around data at the high school in this way:

> It used to be, "Here's the data. Let's move on." To now, "Here's the data, what is it telling us? What's our action plan? What are we doing next to make sure that all the students in the classroom meet the benchmarks and get the support needed?"

Previously, data were used to tell Revere educators how the students performed, but now the data help Revere educators reflect on their performance, as they make ongoing instructional adjustments based on their analysis of what does and does not work for their students.

Leadership Actions to Support Data Use

The process of turning data into actionable information requires time and practice, in addition to a place to store the data. In these very successful schools, the leaders took a number of steps to support effective data use. School leaders in these schools supported effective data use, first and foremost, by clearly identifying the learning and behavioral goals they wanted students to accomplish. Having the goals clearly in mind helped educators determine what kinds of information they needed in order to assess whether students were achieving the goals. Leaders also created time in the daily schedule for teachers to collaborate, articulate and create their subjects' curriculum, daily activities and lessons. This specified what was to be learned and when and how concepts would be taught. To monitor student progress toward the desired goals, leaders required a system of frequent assessment. While most of the districts provided benchmark or interim assessments, teachers further developed common formative assessments and adopted other strategies like exit tickets that assessed the daily learning objective. Planning meetings then naturally included the discussion of data. It was part of the normal routine, not something that happened only after results brought school-wide problems to their attention.

Leaders had to put the system and process in place and then get teachers to believe that it was critical to invest in the analysis of data. They provided compelling reasons why teachers would want to do this hard work. They explained that teachers' proactive use of data would guide the planning and delivery of instruction in ways that would lead more students to mastery the first time a lesson was taught. It was not about state accountability, but rather to help children. Data were not used for autopsy (after the school year ended to determine what went wrong), but rather as vital sign feedback to guide the instructional process toward healthy learning outcomes for all students. In this way, data became embedded in daily practices.

Understanding that teachers needed to be comfortable openly discussing student results and working together to improve teaching and learning, leaders helped encourage a climate of trust among teachers around the use of data. They emphasized data was not to punish or judge, but to help them know the impact of their instruction. Transparency in practice and results was for the benefit of students and the development of staff. To gain maximum benefit from information on student learning, they wanted teachers to discuss their own challenges and concerns, observe each other's lesson and share suggestions on how to improve. According to the O'Farrell teachers we interviewed, teachers are more likely to develop this comfort level if they view their colleagues as teammates, not competitors. "We really rely on each other to help accomplish student goals . . . We show up every day and give our hundred percent every day and help each other get to that point too." An Eastlake teacher expressed a similar sentiment:

> I think what's great is that there is a lot of collegiality between the faculty. Within any department, we get along really well. There is a mixture of veteran and relatively new teachers. There are a lot of great ideas being shared across the board, and you see many similarities across classrooms. There is co-teaching, co-planning, and students getting really great instruction in the classroom.

One English teacher at Pace talked about learning new strategies and techniques from colleagues in other departments after seeing how strong their assessment data was in comparison to her own:

> We try to take ideas from both math and history and incorporate them into our [English] classrooms. I think that's something that others schools may be lacking, because not only are we trying to collaborate within our department or grade level, but with other departments, too . . . I'm already trying to figure out what I'm going to do next year, based on what I've done that maybe wasn't or was successful. How can I make it even better? So, I look at what is the math department doing? What is history doing? What is science doing? Why are they so successful?

Types of Evidence-Based Decision Making

Educators in all four of the schools aimed to make evidence-based decisions, however, the process is not simple or straightforward. Most of our schools said as much, and most had goals to continue to improve their use of data. For example, the academic coach at O'Farrell who said data were everything described her desire to help her colleagues improve their use of data:

One goal I have is around data literacy. I want to help our teachers become researchers in their classrooms and think like researchers. I want to help them use data to inform their instruction in meaningful ways and personalize instruction in a way that accelerates all students' academic achievement.

O'Farrell, like many schools, has a number of online programs to support core instruction. These tools extract data to help create student groups for re-teaching and to inform instruction. But helping teachers make sense of these data along with their formative and benchmark assessments is an ongoing process. In each of the schools, the leaders understood the value of data, but getting the right data, in the right format, at the right time, for the right audience to maximize its impact can be challenging and required a full team effort. Most schools had a data specialist who organized the data and helped lead its use, but it was part of the fabric of each of the schools and something they were always reflecting on. However, teachers had to work together as a team to understand and use the data effectively. "We're very blessed," explained a teacher at Eastlake:

Mr. Gomez is like a wizard with Excel. He gives us reports that are amazing. You can almost pinpoint down to exactly what you need to focus on. I think one of the neatest things is that we have a lot of strengths within our team. What I can't do, he could do and vice versa. That is very helpful.

Across the schools we studied, we found that educators used data to 1) measure individual student learning and progress; 2) create targeted interventions; 3) drive instruction and curriculum development; 4) measure program effectiveness; 5) promote accountability; and 6) allocate resources (see Figure 6.1). In the next section, we offer examples of these six core data-use practices. Our goal is to illuminate how these practices helped teachers more deeply understand their practice—what is working, what can be improved, and what to examine next.

We believe, when it comes to improving instruction and learning, it's not the quantity of the data that counts, but how the information is used (Hamilton et al., 2009). Data are only guideposts, they do not provide answers and solutions. But, when teachers embed regular data collection

Figure 6.1 Six Core Data Use Practices

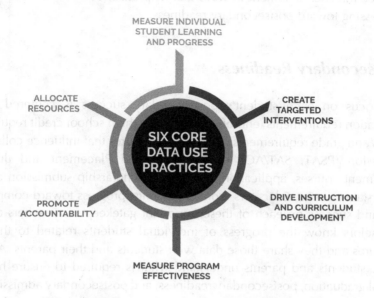

and analysis into their practice to help inform their professional judgment, they are more likely to be guided by evidence than opinion. As one teacher at O'Farrell explained,

> We're using programs like Illuminate to compare data. So it's not just, 'Oh, this works for me because it was really fun.' Instead we look at student results and identify strengths. There's a lot of data . . . but it's balanced. Teachers are allowed to use their intuition, but it has to be backed up with data and student success.

Data to Track and Measure Individual Progress and Success

As we have discussed, educators at each of the four schools, focus on individual student success. At more typical schools, the focus on individual students might be a common sentiment, but not a common practice. In these four schools, however, the regular use of data helps ensure that practice matches sentiment in ways that help ensure that each student is progressing toward postsecondary readiness.

Postsecondary Readiness

The focus on each student's postsecondary success is centered on graduation requirements (end-of-course exams, high school credit requirements and grade requirements), as well as measures that influence college admission (PSAT, SAT/ACT exams, Advanced Placement and dual-enrollment courses, application, FAFSA and scholarship submission and other state criteria). Educators monitor students' progress toward completion and success on each of these important gatekeepers. Teachers and counselors know the progress of individual students related to these measures and they share those data with students and their parents. As a result, students and parents understand what is required to ensure high school graduation, postsecondary readiness, and postsecondary admission. In more typical schools, Latino students and parents might not know about these requirements until they receive notice that the student will not graduate on time or that the student will not be able to attend one of their state's four-year public universities. In contrast, at Eastlake, O'Farrell, Pace, and Revere, students and parents know their status related to graduation and college readiness throughout their high school career.

While the gatekeeper data points (e.g., SAT tests, high school graduation requirements, end-of-course tests) are important, educators in the four schools recognize that many other data points serve as leading indicators (indicators that suggest whether or not students are on track). By focusing upon leading indicators, educators were able to increase the likelihood that their students would perform well on the major, summative indicators.

Tracking Attendance

One key leading indicator is attendance. Students are much more likely to succeed if they attend school regularly. All of the schools tracked attendance data to determine school-wide average daily attendance and to determine each individual student's rate of school attendance. Each of the four schools maintained an average daily attendance rate in excess of 92 percent. This far exceeds the rate at some urban high schools where the average daily attendance is less than 80 percent of the students enrolled. Achieving a high rate of attendance is not easy at urban high schools that serve low-income communities.

At Pace, for example, educators invest considerable time and attention in tracking the attendance of individual students. Many Pace students travel on a couple of buses each day. Some students cross the border and then take a city bus in Brownsville to get to school in the morning. Some Pace students have responsibility for getting their siblings to their elementary and middle schools. One of Pace's assistant principals, Carla Gonzales, compiles and manages a wide array of student data. When asked what data she monitors, the first thing that came up was attendance. She described attendance as "data 101." She and her colleagues monitor how many times a student has been absent and they try to intervene quickly. She explained that the first "line of defense" is first- and second-period teachers. If students are not in class, school personnel call home and talk with parents about getting kids to school. Second, the principal runs reports by grade level and also will call parents. Pace personnel want families to hear from multiple staff members about how much they want their student in school. As well, staff members round up students who have been tardy during lunch and have talks with them. If a student has excessive absences, the educators develop a contract with the student and the student's parents are notified.

Pace educators know that strong attendance requires a team effort, they know that parents care about their children's educational success, but Pace educators realize that parents might not know how they can support their child's regular school attendance. Pace leaders explained that Latino parents see educators as experts and are more than willing to work with them, but often parents need to be engaged with a particular responsibility. So, Pace educators go out of their way to communicate with families about expectations and how parents can help.

Sometimes, parental support is not a sufficient solution. For instance, some parents may have work schedules that prevent them from being able to supervise their children getting to school. There may be transportation or other issues that make attendance more difficult. Leaders at Pace will try to understand the specific problems and create tailored solutions. A key component of the process is talking with students about why it is important that they are in school, and learning about the issues that make regular attendance challenging. Pace leaders make clear to students that they care and will do whatever it takes to support them and their learning.

Some Pace students enroll after having experienced years of academic failure in other schools. Poor attendance may be due to the student's perception that they are not likely to succeed. Some students may be older than their peers and feel out of place. Based on the issues and needs identified, Pace educators respond creatively. For example, for students in situations where traditional transportation solutions were not working, a team went out and picked students up, as needed. Pace leaders allocated resources to accommodate this need and focused on building relationships with students so students would want to be in school and understand the purpose and value of the education they will receive.

In response to a different situation, on the day of our visit, Mr. Leal, a Pace assistant principal was discussing with a student and his parent why the student did not report to class, even though he was at school. Mr. Leal helped the parent and other support staff create an action plan. They decided to not impose excessive consequences because they did not want to push the student further away from school. School security were going meet the student in the hallway, check in with him, and make sure he got to class on time. His parent was also willing to bring him to school and walk him to class if necessary. The team clarified the expectations and surrounded the student with care to provide a tight safety net.

Research consistently documents that Latino students are more likely than other students to drop out of school. Low attendance is a leading indicator of dropout issues. The staff at Pace take this quite seriously (some because of their similar experiences as students). As a result, dropout rates at Pace (as well as Eastlake, O'Farrell, and Revere) are dramatically lower than typical for urban high schools that serve Latino youth.

Special Needs of English Learners on the Path to Graduation

English learners represent a segment of the Latino population at each of the four high schools studied. National data consistently documents extremely low graduation rates for English learners, about 63 percent compared to the national average of 82 percent. And, only about 1 percent take the ACT or SAT college entrance exam. Educators at each of the study high schools want to help their English learner students both graduate and become bilingual and biliterate. One of the ways they promote bilingualism is by tracking students' development of English language proficiency. For example, the EL population is a top priority for O'Farrell. In particular, educators focus upon students who have been designated as English learners for several years (often throughout their elementary and middle school years) and who have not yet been reclassified as English proficient. Educators know that although these students speak conversational English fluently, often, these students struggle with academic language development.

O'Farrell educators want to ensure they provide the right instruction to close the gaps experienced by long-term English learners. They know these students have different needs than students who recently arrived in the U.S. and are just beginning the process of English instruction. Teachers analyze data from their annual administration of the California English Language Development Test (CELDT) to monitor student progress in listening, speaking, reading, and writing in English. The Academic Coordinator organizes the data, looks at strengths, weakness and progress made by each student, and then decides how to intervene for individual students.

As a result, O'Farrell educators have focused on content-specific academic vocabulary in courses and classrooms. Teachers have also identified "power words" by grade level and all students learn eight words per month. Teachers help students become familiar with the vocabulary and integrate it into their spoken language. In contrast to some high school classes where teachers tend to lecture and expect students to sit quietly and listen, O'Farrell teachers deliberately push students to utilize critical vocabulary in conversations. O'Farrell educators have learned that these strategies have been beneficial in promoting the success of all their students, including students who may speak non-standard English or who may not hear academic English at home. Educational strategies that work for English learners are often helpful for other students who might find the language experienced at school surprisingly foreign.

Goal Setting with Students

At all four high schools, educators used data to motivate students. Educators discussed students' individual data with them in ways that helped students establish personal educational goals. For example, many teachers helped

149

students keep track of their learning progress with online gradebooks or tracking sheets. The teachers wanted to empower students by involving them in assessing and reflecting on their own learning. Students' perceptions about their own growth and progress can be powerful tools for tailoring instruction to meet individual needs, so teachers reviewed data with individual students and worked with students to help them set goals and determine strategies for pursuing those goals.

In particular, educators helped students set goals and monitor their progress toward passing important assessments that influenced access to postsecondary education. For example, Texas offers the Texas Success Initiative Assessment, or TSI. The TSI includes three separate exams: mathematics, reading, and writing. Students cannot begin earning credit for college courses until they pass the TSI. By passing the TSI exams, students can avoid remedial classes in community college or state universities. Also, by passing the TSI before high school graduation, students can participate in dual-enrollment offerings and earn both high school and college credit. Both Pace and Eastlake provide students multiple opportunities to take the test. Educators at both school help students track their progress so that all students pass the assessment prior to high school graduation.

Similarly, Revere educators help their students keep track of how well they are negotiating the college and career pathway. They use Naviance, a software tool that provides K-12 schools with college planning and career assessment tools. Counselors use the software to help students explore their interests and strengths and develop a course of study that matches long-term goals with an actionable plan. This plan helps students (and counselors) monitor their progress related to graduation requirements, performance on state assessments, advanced placement classes, electives, intervention classes, internships and dual-enrollment courses.

And, O'Farrell educators track and monitor student progress toward completing the University of California and California State University A-G requirements (courses students are required to complete in high school if they want to attend a state college or university in California). These courses are generally not required for graduation in California, but O'Farrell has set this higher standard to ensure their students are both eligible and ready for postsecondary study.

At all four schools, the determination to ensure that each and every student will be successful has led educators to monitor and analyze data at the individual student level and to include students in that process. This is done both to catch students who are falling off track and to identify goals and celebrate success along the path to postsecondary readiness.

Data to Track Instructional Effectiveness

In addition to assessing individual progress and success, teachers systematically and routinely examine classroom data to guide their instructional decisions and create groups for intervention and enrichment. Teachers use student-learning data as feedback about their instructional practice. When data suggest that students are not learning, teachers do not assume that students are at fault or have limited capacity. Instead, teachers see student mastery data as feedback on their instruction. Educators examine the data to determine which students mastered the material, which did not and how they might modify their instructional strategies to ensure all students master the concept.

Further, teachers compare their outcomes to their colleagues who are teaching the same content or course. PLCs or the teachers' common planning times (as discussed in Chapter Four) are structured to facilitate the thoughtful use of data to generate lesson ideas that maximize student success. By working as teams to examine student data, teachers inquire about and learn from each other's successes. Teachers help each other adopt collective expectations for students' performance, share effective practices, gain a deeper understanding of students' needs and develop effective strategies to better serve students. As well, when weaknesses are identified or teachers identify new strategies they think may be useful, teams may request professional development or provide professional development to each other in ways that build their capacity.

Collaborative teacher inquiry is an important element of the success of these schools. Not only does collaboration lead to new ideas for professional development, but it also leads to careful attention to the effective implementation of professional development concepts in class-rooms. Often, implementation of new strategies is not a smooth process. Teachers may need multiple opportunities to practice, receive feedback, refine implementation, and examine student data before they are able to use strategies effectively and efficiently. In these high-performing high schools, teachers support each other so that data usage, collaboration, professional development and feedback are intertwined in ways that help teachers improve instruction continuously.

Multiple Levels of Analysis

Assessment for learning happens at many levels in these schools: the classroom (e.g., class projects, writing assignments, exit tickets, quizzes), school (e.g., common formative assessments for courses, grades), and the district (e.g., benchmark assessments). And, the data can come from formal sources (written assessments) or from data collected during instruction (teacher observations). For example, a teacher at Eastlake discussed instructional feedback data in this way:

> We process data almost immediately every period. "What's his strength? What's yours?" And we tweak instruction every period. We are actually grouped into grade level sections like the sophomores are in one area, freshman teachers in another. So, for my team, we're all within four doors of each other so we meet every period just informally, but we tweak throughout the day and make adjustments for the benefit of the students.

The teachers in these schools use data from all of these levels to help them reflect upon and improve instruction. By examining and discussing patterns in the data, teachers identify strengths and weaknesses for possible re-teaching, they determine which students are ready for enrichment and which students need interventions, they pinpoint the instructional targets that should be the focus of those interventions and they develop plans for improving instruction in the next unit.

In all four schools, educators used data from common formative assessments (created at the school level) and common benchmark assessments (created at the district level) as tools to improve the effectiveness of instruction. While common formative assessments and other formative assessment processes helped teachers work together to refine instruction weekly, daily, or even in the moment of instructional delivery, benchmark assessments provided another tool for improving instruction quarterly or at a few critical points during the school year. Educators used benchmark assessments to pursue the same purposes: better understanding of what was working and what wasn't working and better understanding of instructional next steps. However, benchmark assessment data provide different opportunities for understanding.

For example, at Eastlake, teachers administer benchmark assessments from the district that are based on state standards and are aligned to the state test taken at the end of the year. The benchmark assessments are given in the fall and spring. An Eastlake educator described the benchmark assessments by saying:

> Those [benchmark assessments] are district-wide so that gives us an assessment of how we are doing across the district. The same grade level across the district will take the same test. It's developed by a team at the district. (It's actually a team of teachers.) We can see how we fare across the district, and then, that data gives us a lot of feedback about standards as well.

The educator continued by explaining how Eastlake teachers analyzed the benchmark data to determine which standards students had mastered and which standards had not been mastered. This information was used to plan once-per-week tutoring interventions and Saturday school programs designed to help students learn the concepts embedded in the standards they had not yet mastered. The educator explained:

> Then, we analyze that data and that is how we create our intervention programs to suit those kid's individual strengths and weaknesses. So, we have planned 11 weeks this semester for students. They are getting tutored in each of the four disciplines and those are once a week. We are also conducting Saturday school and blitzes within the next couple of weeks.

Revere teachers reported a very similar process at their school. They administer quarterly assessments that are standard specific. The teachers receive item-by-item data so they can assess each student's mastery of specific concepts and standards. Also, the data allow the teachers to determine how classes and grade levels performed. A Revere educator explained, "This facilitates discussions about the standards, where we need to improve our teaching, or maybe are there certain strategies we need to rethink, as they are not working."

Although data analysis and application are an integral part of operations at Revere, the superintendent told us one of their district-wide initiatives was examining their assessment practices. They have a goal focused on assessment for student learning that is part of their five-year plan. They plan to better understand best data practices and determine what and how they want to improve. Dr. Kelly explained, "This is part of our five-year plan, but the focus this year is really taking inventory of what kind of assessment practices teachers are actually using in the classroom. And, they're also writing a core value statement." The value statement is intended to clarify their beliefs about grading and the role of assessment in the learning process for students.

In spite of their many successes and accolades, Revere teachers (like teachers in other high-performing urban schools) tended to be critical of themselves. In developing their core value statement, teachers noted, "Student grades were a matter of geography." They challenged themselves to improve the link between the grade given and the mastery of concepts and ensure that the same work would generate the same grade across classes. And, like the example given at the start of the chapter, they wanted to review other practices and their impact on students. In particular, they were looking at homework and homework grading practices and evaluating if they were fair to students.

One Revere teacher said they knew they had many Latino students,

> ... who leave school and go to work and work until two o'clock in the morning and get four hours sleep at night, three nights a week. They have to do this to support their family. How can we be asking that kid, "Get me your homework tomorrow" the same way we're asking the child who's going to go home, take a nap, have a snack that mom left for them, eat dinner with their family and go to bed early. Do you know what I mean? We have to make allowances for kids so that we're really giving them the opportunity that they need to show us what they know.

Analysis of Programs and Interventions

Educators also used data to evaluate programs and new strategies being implemented to improve teaching and learning. For example, schools often broke down data by different student groups to ensure there was equal access to programs and opportunities. In particular, all four schools were attempting to increase access to the most rigorous courses the school offered, including AP and dual-enrollment courses. Dr. Garcia, at Revere, was emphatic that increases in access would be equitable for Latino and English learner students. He described the data by explaining:

> Since 2009, we've more than doubled the number of kids who are taking AP courses, right? So you would say big deal. You just said that you doubled your student population from 900 to 1,800, right? So it makes sense, but when you keep in mind that our demographics have changed so significantly to the point that 43 percent of our kids are Hispanic and only 37 percent are White, you see that those new kids who are taking the AP classes are Hispanic kids.

One way that Revere educators ensured equal access to AP was to offer an ESL AP Literature class. Rather than waiting for students to proceed through all the English learner levels and running out of time to take an AP class, they created an AP class specifically for English learners. When conducting focus groups with students, Mrs. Chan, the ESL AP literature teacher was often named the students' best or favorite teacher. For example, one student said:

> My favorite class is math in general. I really love numbers and all that. But my favorite teacher is Ms. Chan. She's my English teacher. She teaches us AP literature. It's an opportunity that they're giving to us this year and I feel proud of myself.

Another student followed by saying:

> My favorite teacher would be Ms. Chan also. She dedicates so much of herself to her students. That's something I appreciate and since the beginning of the year we have

learned so much stuff that I had no idea we would have access to.

In addition to using data to ensure program access, educators at the four schools used data to ensure that they were implementing programs well. For example, during the 2016–17 school year, O'Farrell educators were working to improve their students' critical reading skills. The teachers participated in professional development to better understand critical reading skills and worked together to strategize what changes they might make to improve students' ability to be critical readers and to consider how the text portrays the subject matter. However, they also wanted to know if their new classroom strategies designed to improve critical reading skills made a difference for their students. One teacher explained:

> We were expected as a department to do a PDSA cycle—
> plan-do-study-act. And so as a department, department chairs
> led their team in deciding what strategy they were going to
> implement in their department. They studied the data, they
> implemented the strategy, they studied the data again and
> then we actually had a presentation, kind of like a conference
> style, like breakout-session style, where other teachers could
> go around and watch each other's presentations, learning
> about the strategies being done in different departments and
> their effects. So there is creativity to try new things, but then
> also data that brings you back to, did this work, what kind
> of changes are we going to need to make to achieve the
> outcome we want?

This example also shows how learning is spread throughout the campus. In addition to examining feedback about their own implementation and its impact, staff benefitted from learning about the choices other staff and departments made that might help them improve their own choices.

Data for Accountability

Accountability data are often perceived as negative as they are often used to judge schools and educators. Often accountability data are presented as ratings and rankings, without context. Educators in many urban schools tend to see accountability data as political mechanisms intended to prove the futility of improvement efforts. But for these four schools, accountability data were perceived differently. Like data to improve teaching and learning, accountability data provided another signal of progress toward the goals that educators held for their students. State expectations for performance provided a tool that allowed educators to compare their progress to other similar schools or to compare themselves to more affluent schools, the real target as educators sought to close achievement gaps for their Latino, low-income and English learner students.

Dr. Dean, the superintendent of O'Farrell reflected, "Charter schools live and die by their data." At O'Farrell, he explained that they constantly keep track of their data and examine what the data suggest about their performance. His goal is for O'Farrell students to compete successfully with any students in the county, state, or across the country. O'Farrell educators are not satisfied to outperform schools that serve a similar population of students. Their goal is to prepare students to be successful upon graduation. Recent data indicate that O'Farrell high school students outperform most high school students in San Diego city and county, including some of the most affluent schools in the area. They use these data as external reference points and are open to what the data suggest. For example, when we asked what he wanted to improve at O'Farrell, Principal Rainey responded:

> Math. Like everybody. We do well in math, but, it's all relative. We do well, comparatively. Overall, everybody's struggling with the new Common Core Math . . . Now, it's like, if you have 35 percent of your kids at the proficient level, you're like, "Wow. We did pretty well." Which is so horrible! It's so hard for me to see that and go, "That's good." You know, we still did better than the state average, the county average, and the San Diego Unified average. But we're really struggling to become really high performing in math. We're going to do it. I've got the people to do it.

Similarly, Principal Longoria at Pace reflected on her accountability data. She was very proud of her school earning six of seven state

157

distinctions. Even more so, she was proud that they met all safeguards for the student groups the state considered "at risk." As she said:

> This is something to be very, very proud of. You see these [strong, positive] numbers in many elementary schools, but it is very hard to find these [strong, positive] numbers in a high school. We owe it all to the work that the teachers do . . . The systems are there and the teachers follow them with fidelity.

Principal Martinez also reflected on his school's accountability data and the signal it provided to him and his Eastlake staff. Like Pace, Eastlake earned six of seven distinctions. This clearly indicated where they needed to focus and improve. One administrator said:

> ELAR (English Language Arts/Reading) was one of the distinctions we missed at this campus. Of course, the English department does take that to heart because we want to make sure we make enough gains to push us over, so that we can make the seventh distinction. The pressure is on. We want to make sure it's collaborative with everyone in the school. One of our first trainings campus-wide was writing across the curriculum. We make sure that our science department, our social studies department and our math department have new ways for incorporating reading and writing in their classrooms.

The data in this case provided some motivation and triggered a competitive spirit to improve. But, Eastlake educators didn't just point fingers at the English department, they thought through how the whole school could collaborate to improve outcomes for their students. The data provided a reminder that there was more to do. Even though Eastlake students performed above the state average, there was more work to do so their students were performing with the very best students. Similarly, Mr. Martinez, the principal reflected on what he saw in the data:

> When you start looking at my SPED (Special Education) numbers, I think my SPED program needs to improve. We

need to do something differently. All of my incoming special education students are served in what they would call a resource class at the middle school. And when they come to high school they want to continue in resource. You're not going to learn it [the standards] there. So I'm going to fully immerse them as much as possible in mainstream classes. We'll make sure that we're in compliance, but we're going to put them in regular classes so they learn the same standards.

The leaders in these schools welcome accountability data and the feedback it provides them. They do not look at results and say the test is flawed or it was a bad day for the kids. They know there are limitations with assessments, but they strive to be open to the feedback it provides them. Leaders are also careful to avoid using data to blame educators or students. Instead, they work with educators to find solutions that will help ensure the success of every student. Educators at all four schools use external state accountability data as a means of comparison that their internal data cannot provide. Their success on one measure emboldens them to assume that they can and should be successful on other measures. Their progress with one student group leads them to believe that they should be able to make progress for every student group.

Figure 6.2 Key Considerations to Build a Data Use Culture

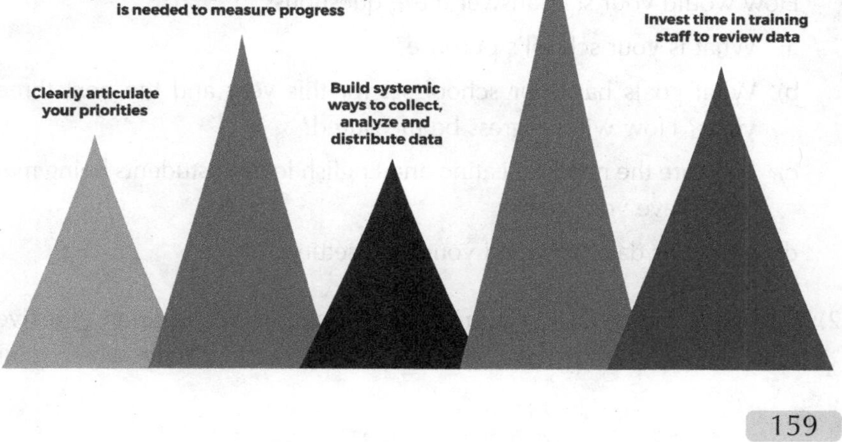

Provide time and space to discuss data

Determine what data and at what level (student, classroom, course or school) is needed to measure progress

Invest time in training staff to review data

Clearly articulate your priorities

Build systemic ways to collect, analyze and distribute data

Conclusion

For many, data are confusing or intimidating. And, most would say, schools are drowning in data. Indeed, planning and collecting strong and reliable data and using it effectively to support the school's vision and goals is a demanding process. In all four schools, the culture of data use did not develop overnight or remain static each year. Figure 6.2 outlines key actions to build a data use culture. The teachers needed practice and each school dedicated time and training to help the staff use data in meaningful ways. Each of these schools had to consider its priorities and build systematic ways to collect, analyze, and distribute data aligned with their priorities to teachers, students, and parents. Data to understand and support individual students was of utmost importance. Including students in data tracking and analysis was a key part of this process.

As well, teachers used student learning data as feedback for improving their instruction. At all four schools, the alignment between state standards, curricula, instruction and assessment grew stronger as collaborative teams worked together to ensure that they were teaching what students needed to learn and as they sought to ensure that their instruction was leading students to learn what they endeavored to teach. In all of this, leadership was essential to establish a clear, constructive vision for school-wide data use, provide supports that fostered a data-driven culture, and to make data part of the ongoing cycle of instructional improvement.

Self-Assessment

1) Leadership nurtures a culture of data use and provides a guiding vision. How would your staff answer these questions?

   a) What is your school's purpose?

   b) What goals has your school set for this year and the next three years? How will progress be measured?

   c) How are the needs of Latino and English learner students being met to achieve your goals?

   d) How has data informed your goal setting?

2) Some systems need to be in place for schools to create an effective data use culture. Review the systems below and evaluate where your

school is at with implementation (Poor, Fair, Good, Very Good, Excellent).

a) There are systems in place to ensure data from common assessments are reported to teachers, coaches, and administrators in a timely manner.

b) There is a template for reporting and disaggregating common assessment data in ways that make the data actionable.

c) There are systems in place to ensure teachers have time to meet to review data, identify strengths and needs, and plan improvement strategies to address the needs of students.

d) There is a data inquiry protocol to help teachers with the analysis of data.

e) There is a data guru or someone who has overall responsibility for data coordination and use on your campus.

f) Multiple types of data are used to understand student needs and progress towards goals.

g) New programs or initiatives are monitored with data.

h) Accountability data are shared and discussed.

3) There are some educational practices that are necessary to be in place for schools to be able to maximize data use. Review the practices below and assess what percent of your teachers are engaged in these practices:

a) What percent of teachers in the same academic area (e.g., English I or Algebra) have a clear, shared understanding of what mastery of each priority standard should look like?

b) What percent of teachers regularly use checking-for-understanding strategies during instruction to ensure that each student is making progress toward mastery?

c) What percent of teachers administer regular and frequent common formative assessments to monitor students' progress toward mastery?

References

Chenoweth, K., & Theokas, C. (2011). *Getting it done: Leading academic success in unexpected schools*. Cambridge, MA: Harvard Education Press.

Edmonds, R. (1979). Effective schools for the urban poor. *Educational Leadership*, *37*, 15–24.

Hamilton, L., et al. (2009). *Using student achievement data to support instructional decision making (NCEE 2009–4067)*. Washington, DC: National Center for Education Evaluation and Regional Assistance, Institute of Education Sciences, U.S. Department of Education.

Johnson, J. F., Uline, C. L., & Perez, L. G. (2017). *Leadership in America's best urban schools*. New York: Routledge.

Conclusion

Developing Schools that Succeed with Latino Students

I don't think there are a lot of schools like our school, to be honest.

—Student, Pace Early College High School

The last question we asked all stakeholder groups during our visits to each school was, "If there was one thing you wanted us to remember about your school, what would it be?" The responses we received were quite powerful and captured the essence of the schools (see Table 7.1). Responses were quite similar across stakeholder groups and also across the schools. The responses emphasized elements of care and love for the students; a sense of team or family; ambitious expectations and transformational opportunities; and a commitment to continuous improvement and success for all students. So, although we agree with the student quoted at the start of the chapter (that there are not a lot of urban high schools like her school), the four schools we studied represent what we want for our children. These are schools that have figured out how to 1) provide a rich and challenging curricula to all students, 2) engage students in instruction that is personalized to respond to their strengths and needs, and 3) create a school culture that is focused on continuous improvement and designed to ensure that all stakeholders (especially students) feel connected, cared about, valued and respected. The result is that their students are prepared for college, careers and civic life. They provide hope for urban education and affirm that equity and excellence are possible.

The successes of these four schools occur against a backdrop of sobering national data for Latino students. So, ultimately, we hoped to understand what educators did at these four schools to generate powerful changes in learning outcomes. We learned that they did not design a

Table 7.1 Representative Responses from School Staff,
Students and Parents About Their School

School	What do you want us to remember about your school response?
Eastlake High School	I think one of the big things is this ideology that failure is not an option. There is a willingness to not stop, not to quit, to keep going, whatever obstacle we may have.
The O'Farrell High School	This is a place of opportunity; if you come here it is very, very difficult to not succeed. You have cheerleaders and mentors and a support system. There's a safety net here that you just can't fall through.
Pace Early College High School	There are opportunities for every kid, at every level, every day at Pace. And, with those opportunities every day, we are going to close the learning gap.
Revere High School	I would say reflection. I think that whether the change comes quickly or slowly, we are constantly trying to look at what we're doing and trying to make adjustments to it and trying to improve on it. We want what is best for students.

special program or intervention that catered specifically to the needs of Latino students. They did not purchase a special technological approach or adopt a unique professional development program. Instead, they focused squarely on the needs, strengths, and interests of all the student they served. The meticulous focus grew out of a powerful belief that all of their students could achieve high levels of academic success, if educators provided the right supports and opportunities.

This emphasis on each and every student did not blind educators to the special needs and strengths of Latino students or English learners. True, their Latino students often needed additional support to become fluent in English and the educators actively considered, valued, and included Latino culture in the school environment, but the overarching perspective was both individualized, positive, and strengths-based. Educators did not approach their work thinking about remediating perceived deficits; the school environment was purposely additive, rather than subtractive (Valenzuela, 1999). Educators believed their students deserved a quality education and expected the best from themselves as they worked together

164

to tailor schedules, routines, classes, instructional strategies, support structures and other school elements in ways that would maximize the success of each student. As well, educators expected the best from their students regardless of racial/ethnic stereotypes, academic levels, family socio-economic levels, language proficiency, or disability. As a result, their students' futures are full of promise as educators help students reach their goals and aspirations.

Before summarizing the most important takeaways from our research, we want to remind readers that these high schools have non-selective admissions and serve predominantly low-income student populations. All of the schools had a majority of Latino students and all had significant populations of English learners. The challenges they faced were real and significant and the work was not easy, but with planning and intentionality, we believe these outcomes are possible in far more schools. We hope their

Figure 7.1 Five Key Practices of Successful Schools

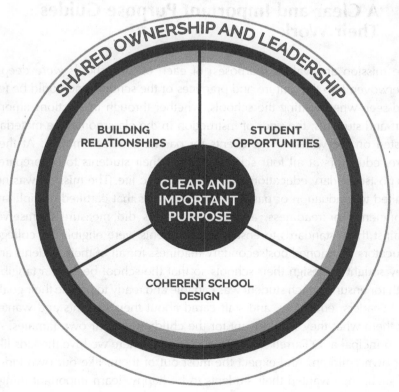

stories inspire, but also point to five specific actions other committed educators can take in their schools (see figure 7.1).

The five things we want you to remember about these schools are:

1) A clear and important purpose guides their work.

2) Building relationships among staff and students is a priority.

3) Opportunities for students are rich and extensive.

4) A coherent school design supports teachers and students to achieve their goals.

5) There is shared ownership and leadership to accomplish the work.

These five practices are part of an integrated strategy that led to each school's success.

A Clear and Important Purpose Guides Their Work

The mission and values (purposes) of each of the schools were deeply interwoven into the culture and practices of the schools and could be felt and seen when visiting the schools, whether through interactions among staff and students, the rigor of instruction in the classrooms, the materials posted on the walls, or the events for parents and community. At their core, educators at all four schools wanted their students to be prepared for postsecondary education, careers, and civic life. The mission was not limited to graduation or passing external exams that certified disciplinary proficiency or readiness, although educators did measure themselves against these standards to ensure their students were eligible for college. Educators envisioned postsecondary readiness for all of their students and they sought to design their schools so that the school became a tangible path for ensuring each student was capable and ready to pursue their goals.

Leaders, educators, and staff cared about their students and wanted for them what they would want for the children in their own families. As the principal at O'Farrell said, "This is a place where we love the kids like our own children. And expect the most out of them, like our own kids." As such, they wanted their students to be happy, learn important things, pursue their interests and not be limited by any barriers the world might throw at them. They were acutely aware that other schools underserved their Latino, low-income, and English learner students and they were adamant that was not going to be the case at their school. For their students to gain access to the opportunities their more privileged peers enjoyed, educators knew they needed to provide an education that was rich and broadly defined. They did not narrow or water down the curriculum or provide "drill and kill" instruction. They passionately believed in the capacity of their students and felt personally accountable for ensuring they received an enriching education that opened doors. This was the larger purpose that motivated the staff and made them feel their work was valuable and worthwhile.

Although school staff shared the vision and ensured it was enacted in daily decisions and choices, school leaders had a special responsibility in ensuring that was the case. As mentioned in Chapter Two, anyone can write a vision statement articulating a beautiful future for their students and school, but it requires leadership to create a shared vision that resonates with staff, is relevant and feels meaningful and doable by everyone. The ability to articulate a vision that is both inspiring and credible means the school leader must help people find meaning in their work by linking it to the higher purpose. We found the school mottos were one of the ways the leader did this. As brands, "together, we're better," or "we are educating students, graduating leaders and empowering the community" were powerful motivators and helped shape a unity of purpose. Leaders helped staff feel part of something larger than their specific course or role. But, they also recognized each person's contribution to that purpose (through their course, discipline or role at the school) and why it was meaningful. Leaders did this by talking with staff about the students and school, asking them their ideas about what they thought was important and celebrating their individual and collective accomplishments.

Leaders at all four schools expected educators to really know their students, not just their names, but who they were, what their lives were like outside of school, and what their hopes and dreams were. In addition, leaders expected educators to adhere to core values: respecting individual differences, expecting high levels of commitment and effort, valuing teamwork and collaboration, and respecting families as partners in the process. They never blamed students or families for poor outcomes and they did not pity their students, despite the very difficult circumstances some of their students experienced. They understood the difficulties and challenges, but instead of lowering expectations, they reflected on what they could do to ensure students were at school, engaged and learning. They thought about how the school and their system and processes needed to adapt. This clarity regarding goals and values made certain the mission was not fractured and students were not sorted into different tracks with different goals and expectations.

These are truly student-centered schools. Decisions about policies, practices, and procedures were centered upon what educators determined to be best for students. It is important to note that these educators are not martyrs and they don't have special powers. Rather, they take their work seriously, get to know their students, rely on their vision and goals to help make choices, and focus on continuously getting better. They try to translate their convictions into meaningful action that results in positive change and outcomes. Building this culture is not easy work, but having a clear vision and purpose that educators can connect to and believe in goes a long way.

Building Relationships Among Staff and Students is a Priority

There is a very explicit expectation at each of these schools that school faculty build relationships with students, parents, and each other. In particular, leaders and educators believed strongly that students must feel connected to their teachers in order to learn from them. To do the hard work of learning rigorous standards, students need teachers who encourage them through challenges, ignore past failures, break things down into manageable chunks, provide extra help when necessary, and generally just believe in their capabilities. However, this responsibility of relationship building to support learning did not rest solely with teachers. All staff members, irrespective of their roles, were expected to connect with students and form meaningful bonds. This included counselors, coaches, office staff, security personnel and facility managers. A comprehensive team was needed to ensure all students had connections to caring adults at school, had access to the resources and services they needed in order to succeed and had adults who were carefully monitoring their progress to ensure that they did not "fall through the cracks."

In addition to the personal relationships staff cultivated through their roles and interactions with students, leaders also built explicit structures and daily practices to increase the likelihood that staff knew the students and personal and meaningful relationships were formed among staff and students. Some schools used an advisory period, administrators were visible in classrooms and hallways and ate lunch with students, teachers led clubs based on their expertise or interest or coached sports to expand their interactions with students, and student voice and leadership were welcomed in classroom and school decisions.

As well, a culture of celebration supported and strengthened student-centered learning environments. Students were recognized for different types of abilities (e.g., sports, debate, arts, and exemplary schoolwork). Recognition was provided during daily announcements. Outstanding student work, college acceptances, and trophies for curricular and extracurricular accomplishments were displayed on walls and in cabinets. And, in formal and informal interactions, educators regularly recognized students for small and large behaviors and accomplishments. Educators intentionally tried to create a family atmosphere where everyone was welcomed, accepted, and respected. School personnel and students enjoyed each other. They had fun together and shared different experiences. Learning more about one another strengthened connections. All of these efforts to build relationships led students to believe that teachers and staff cared about them and were committed to their success.

Relationships with families were an integral part of the system of personalization and connection that contributed to the schools' successes. School leaders and staff respected families and assumed that parents wanted their children to be successful and that parents would do what they could to support their children's school success, particularly if parents were supported and welcomed as partners in the process. School leaders and staff understood that they were less likely to achieve their goals for student learning if family members did not understand and believe that school personnel had positive intentions for their children's success. Educators nurtured a sense of hope, helping families envision a better future that included college and a variety of careers for their children. Teachers and school staff regularly communicated with parents to build a tight safety net, consistency and common expectations for students. Educators knew parents could not always participate in typical ways or at times most convenient for school personnel, so educators believed it was their responsibility to adapt, rather than to blame. Parents reciprocated by informing the school about issues, asking for help, and advocating for what they believed was in the best interest of their children. Educators were intentional about creating opportunities to get to know families, welcome them on campus, and provide resources they needed. At each school, personnel developed structures, routines, policies, and norms to build connections with families that worked. The goal was to create a community and build and strengthen it in meaningful ways.

Positive relationships were also prevalent among staff members. We saw abundant evidence that teachers liked one another, respected each other's strengths and contributions and generally relied on one another to do the work necessary to be successful. All schools used collaborative teams to organize and structure work around the instructional core, that is the relationship between students, teachers and curriculum (City, Elmore, Fiarman, & Teitel, 2009). Leaders knew teachers, isolated in individual classrooms, were less likely to accomplish ambitious student learning goals, so they made time during the school day for teachers to work with one another, observe each other, identify challenges and solutions, and benefit from one another's expertise. Administrators and support staff attended collaboration meetings, visited classrooms and attended events to support staff, as they pursued shared goals. These interactions helped build a sense of community and commitment to each other's personal and professional success.

Relationships were the basis of the positive learning climate for all stakeholders. But, we want to emphasize, this was not solely about demonstrating care. Educators worked hard to develop relationships with students to build trust, so students would learn more. Students felt valued and capable, so they were willing to work harder and achieve things they never thought possible. Similarly, relationships with colleagues weren't merely about liking one another, but about building trust to work together and collaborate. Deep professional relationships were needed to help teachers learn how to teach challenging standards to all of their students. Educators relied on one another to invest the same effort, prop each other up as needed and share knowledge so they all improved their craft. Staff, in whatever role they held, supported classroom teaching and instruction to ensure students were learning and on-track to reach their goals. Working in high-need urban schools is demanding. Sustaining the hard work necessary to change requires trust and a team committed to the same goals.

Opportunities for Students are Rich and Extensive

In addition to relationships, leaders and educators at these four urban high schools are committed to providing rich and extensive learning opportunities for their students. As mentioned, these are not drill and kill factories. The vision for students is far more extensive. Educators are committed to engagement and deep learning. We found that educators in each school attempted to provide a robust set of experiences for students (that compared favorably to the experiences of students in affluent school communities) and addressed their students' unique interests through curricular, co-curricular, and extra-curricular activities. As well, educators considered and reflected on gaps their students may experience and tried to include those experiences into the school experience including, for example, visits to the beach, museums, colleges and out-of-state or international travel.

First, standards guided an understanding of what students should know and be able to do in the core disciplines. Teachers focused on helping students master priority standards, so their students could effectively participate and compete with students not only in their community, but also throughout the state and country. Educators built enriching lessons and activities into the curriculum to deepen student understanding and provide opportunities for practical application of concepts and provoke critical thinking. All four schools incorporated some block scheduling into their routines to allow deeper exploration of topics. Also, while some students needed intervention, other students were ready for more challenging academic material and were given opportunities to acquire and demonstrate that knowledge. Collaborative teams developed activities and designed lesson plans that required advanced levels of understanding for students who were ready for that level of engagement. In some cases, peer tutors and other supports enhanced proficiency. Next, all schools built access to more rigorous curricula and advanced courses into their schedule and encouraged and prodded as many students as possible into challenging themselves, while providing the additional support they required to engage at that level. All four schools were persistent about adding more advanced courses including both AP and dual-enrollment courses. This was both about ensuring eligibility for competitive post secondary options and giving students a head start on college to help defray the costs that could potentially derail some students.

However, opportunities for students were not just about academic learning in the traditional subjects. The larger comprehensive high schools significantly expanded course opportunities with all sorts of different career pathways for students to explore. These options ranged extensively from the traditional (e.g., culinary arts and cosmetology) to cutting edge STEM fields, such as, aerospace and mechanical engineering. Educators brought in options they knew were relevant to their communities and future job prospects for students, but students also advocated for particular career options that interested them. The goal was to engage students and provide opportunities for students to learn about themselves, their interests, and how they might pursue those pathways after high school.

Co-curricular programs were another avenue for enrichment and helped students to apply their learning in different settings. Students were able to complete internships and engage in different types of teams at school like the math team, debate club, academic decathlons, and future business leader competitions, to name just a few. These opportunities brought students off campus to learn in real world environments and also compete with students from different schools. These experiences provided students new perspectives and a deeper sense of personal efficacy as students recognized their capacity to succeed beyond their school campuses. Often, students enjoyed successful experiences because school personnel believed in them, worked with them, prepared them, and did whatever seemed necessary to support their success.

Finally, educators endeavored to provide students with a well-rounded experience with traditional extra-curricula activities including sports, art, music, and drama. These programs gave students the opportunity to pursue their interests and improve their skills. All of the schools also encouraged the students to give back to their communities and engage in community service. They were loved and cared for at school and staff had high expectations for them, which prompted students to demonstrate similar levels of care and commitment to others in their community.

Schools often cite resources or the master schedule as barriers to creating a rich set of opportunities for students. Sometimes, educators cite the students, saying students need to focus exclusively on only a small set of courses because they do not possess foundational skills. Educators in the four schools studied were creative in thinking about how to expand the opportunities for students. Educators knew if their students did not have access to enriching opportunities, their future opportunities would be limited. Leaders of these four high schools knew that, in spite of the inherent challenges, they had to create a culture that would inspire students (including Latino students from low-income homes) to invest considerable effort, learn, and grow.

A Coherent School Design Supports Teachers and Students to Achieve Their Goals

There have been decades of research on effective schools (Bryk, Sebring, Allensworth, Luppescu, & Easton, 2010; Chenoweth, 2007; Edmonds, 1979; Purkey & Smith, 1983), effective instructional practices (City, Elmore, Fiarman, & Teitel, 2009; Marzano, 2001, 2003; Johnson, Perez, & Uline, 2012) and the necessary elements of effective school leadership (Chenoweth & Theokas, 2013; Johnson, Uline, & Perez, 2017; Leithwood, Louis, Anderson, & Wahlstrom, 2004; Marzano, Waters, & McNulty, 2005). These four urban high schools are reflective of the knowledge gained from those bodies of research, but what sets them apart is the coherent school design that surrounds their practice and 1) supports consistency in instructional effectiveness, and 2) guarantees students' needs are met. Research has documented and confirmed what we have long known: teachers are the most important in-school factor responsible for student achievement. However, research has also underscored the considerable variation in teacher quality across classrooms (Hattie, 2009; Sanders & Rivers, 1996). Further, there is more variation among teachers within schools than across schools (Rivkin, Hanushek, & Kain, 2015). Although we know urban schools, on average, are lower-performing than typical affluent, suburban schools, research recognizes that there are strong teachers in all schools. The challenge schools face is how to bring teacher effectiveness to scale. These four schools have tried to address that challenge as they realize it is the only way they can help all students meet challenging learning standards, including their Latino, low-income, and English learner students.

The coherent school design each school created organizes and anchors the work around the core purpose of the school: student preparation, engagement, and readiness for postsecondary pursuits including college, careers and civic life. Further, we found the alignment between system elements (i.e., the master schedule, teacher collaboration, intervention and enrichment, capacity building, and data use) helps staff learn and feel capable and supports a focus on continuous school improvement. With clarity in goals and data to assess implementation and impact, leaders, educators and staff understood where they needed to improve. Because educators were members of a team with a collective identity and purpose, they were able to support each other in looking critically at what was working and identifying important next steps to advance their progress, rather than acting defeated or demoralized if they didn't achieve their goals. Chapters Four, Five, and Six describe in detail how each of the schools capitalized on traditional structures, components, and elements of high schools to achieve their purposes. There were commonalities across schools, but local context including size of school, resources, and skill level of staff led to variations in implementation (e.g., different master scheduled models). But, ultimately it was the alignment of the elements around their vision of student success that proved to be powerful. This helped them year-by-year to become more explicit about what good educational practice looked like and how to work toward that as a staff.

We want to emphasize three points that helped each school enact their vision. Just having teacher collaboration, professional development, or using data in and of themselves do not lead to the outcomes we found in their schools. One, there was a clear vision that differentiated good, effective teaching from less effective teaching and there was transparency and openness about efforts to support teachers as they worked to implement good teaching practices. As mentioned in Chapter Five, each school adopted a model of what they thought effective instruction looked like. This helped leaders and teachers have a common language with which to reflect upon and discuss what was occurring in classrooms and where changes needed to be made. Teachers developed their curricula and lessons in department and course-alike groups, but there were overarching principles and approaches they were using in common. This provided autonomy and did not constrain pedagogy, enabling teachers to be authentic and to meet the needs of the students in their classroom, while also providing consistency for students across classrooms. Formative and summative assessments provided feedback about what students were learning and how deeply they understood concepts. As well, teachers examined and compared student work to better understand whether assignments were rigorous, how students approached the work, and whether they learned the material.

Second, there were robust systems to support adult learning to enact the instructional vision. Educators did not just talk about what teaching should look like in one professional development session. Teachers had specific professional development goals and participated in ongoing professional development initiatives that were embedded in the everyday work of teachers in classroom. Classroom observations were tailored to allow teacher leaders and administrators to provide feedback about the extent to which the professional development goals were implemented and teachers enjoyed multiple opportunities to visit classrooms where the desired professional practices were being implemented well. The theory of action underlying school-wide efforts was that teachers needed repeated exposure and practice to build new skills and change their instruction in ways that lead to student mastery. And, feedback needed to be specific and actionable. It was ok to struggle; effort and growth were acknowledged and appreciated. Leaders shared responsibility for helping their colleagues succeed and everyone was expected to serve as a leader at some point related to some aspect of teaching. The approaches and actions were intended to help staff understand the practice, discriminate mediocre from excellent implementation, and develop plans for making successive approximations towards the instructional vision of excellent teaching and learning. All four schools embodied a culture of learning: both for students and for adults. They realized implementation of practices was messy and not a linear process, so they provided multiple opportunities and mechanisms for providing feedback and supporting improvement.

Third, despite their best efforts to ensure first instruction lead to student mastery with teacher collaboration and capacity building systems, these schools also had an integrated system of intervention (based on data and teacher knowledge of students) to ensure students had numerous opportunities and avenues to learn the material deeply. They were not satisfied for students to learn the material only to pass the test and never know the concept again. And, assessment processes provided timely information to teachers about exactly what students were learning and where there were gaps in their learning. As a result, they thoughtfully designed systems for extra help, practice, and targeted assistance that were accessible to students and proactive. They did not wait for students to fail. Support mechanisms were built into the school day and extended the school day. Also, student engagement was a priority. Teachers across different subject areas coordinated with one another and afterschool sports and clubs to remove barriers to student participation. Similarly, intervention was a natural part of school, rather than punishment or something that singled out student deficiencies. As a result, students felt teachers cared about their learning. Students believed that their teachers were doing everything they could to ensure their academic success. Therefore, students were more eager to participate and take ownership of their learning.

These coherent school designs were not easy to align, nor were they perfectly implemented from the outset. Each school took the time to build and align them into an interlocking whole. They learned what was effective, what was ineffective, and improved structures according to their goals. As well, they are continuing to evolve and adapt to the changing needs of the staff and students. The main point is that they are not structural changes that do little to improve student achievement, but rather they are designed specifically to address student achievement issues that influence the success of their students. Their commitment that all students learn the same rigorous curriculum requires a thoughtful, coordinated, systematic approach to providing the best first instruction possible so that all students are likely to develop useful understandings of key concepts without intervention or remediation. As well, the coherent school design includes attention to the task of building the capacity of every educator to provide effective, engaging first instruction, as well as provide a thoughtful, timely, coordinated, and systematic response when some students do not learn the material despite the best initial efforts of their teachers.

There is Shared Ownership and Leadership to Accomplish the Work

The final point we would like to make is that creating and sustaining these effective school communities requires substantial investment in developing and supporting staff capacity and distributing leadership widely across the campus. School leaders understand that this work cannot be accomplished alone. Teachers isolated in their classrooms or one superhero principal cannot bring about the changes necessary to ensure all students reach high standards. Everyone in the building has a role that is essential to helping achieve the school goals. The expertise, knowledge, skills and talents of all staff are respected and brought to bear to accomplish the daily work of the school, solve problems and constantly improve. As well, leaders grow leadership throughout the organization by identifying and tapping potential leaders and by creating structures, processes and opportunities for staff to step up and take responsibility for important tasks and goals. None of this can be accomplished without the elements we already discussed including (most importantly) a shared school-wide vision. This helps everyone avoid distractions and focus on the essential improvements. This larger purpose helps staff look beyond the daily issues and see the big picture. Shared commitment and responsibility emerge as everyone is working toward the same outcomes. Teachers work on improving instruction, administrators provide targeted feedback, facility and security personnel ensure the school is safe and welcoming, counselors help students identify their goals and a path to achieving them, and the list goes on.

John Hattie recently updated his list of the most consequential influencers of student achievement and learning in schools (see his address at the Collaborative Impact: Research & Practice Conference in March 2017). Top of that list was teacher collective efficacy. Collective efficacy is the shared perceptions of teachers in a school that the efforts of the faculty as a whole will have positive effects on students (Goddard, Hoy, & Hoy, 2004). These four schools nurtured that belief by valuing and respecting staff, allowing staff to have a voice in identifying priorities and influencing decisions, as well as by opening up classrooms so teachers knew about one another's work and also building effective systems of intervention to ensure students mastered the standards. These actions are concrete ways to begin to build the conditions in your school that lead to shared ownership and leadership. And, to reinforce just how powerful these actions can be, research has documented that the effect of perceived collective efficacy on student achievement was stronger than the link between socioeconomic status and student achievement (Bandura, 1977; Goddard, Hoy, & Hoy, 2000).

Conclusion

The four schools profiled achieved success with all their students and their Latino students in particular. Educators were guided by their core beliefs about education and their passion to do whatever it takes to ensure their students learned. Creating a team that is willing to see things differently and teach differently may seem like a daunting task. But, our experience in successful schools, improving schools, and those schools that haven't figured it out yet, is that they all have passionate educators who want to do the best for their students.

The late Ron Edmonds is reported to have been fond of saying, "If it has been done, it can be done." We are convinced that the successes achieved by educators at these four schools can be achieved by educators at more schools throughout our country. This does not imply that such success is easy or simple. In fact, it requires sustained, focused effort; talented, committed leadership at multiple levels; and a belief in the capacity of all students to succeed that is so strong that it drives a team of stakeholders to identify strengths and needs, examine options for improving practices, build everyone's capacity to implement the practices well, implement the practices, assess the quality of implementation, support improved implementation over time, assess growth in student learning outcomes, and identify new strengths and needs, over and over and over again. And, all of this must be done in a culture that makes students, parents, teachers, and support staff feel valued, respected, appreciated, and capable. But, it can be done. We had the pleasure of studying four impressive schools that are doing it.

Fortunately, we can also report that the rewards are worth the tremendous effort required. We are not referencing the rewards associated with state accountability systems (or the relief from sanctions associated with state accounting systems). Nor do we suggest that the various distinctions provided to these schools by outside entities (such as our America's Best Urban Schools Award) make the considerable effort worthwhile. We know that the effort is worthwhile because we had the pleasure of talking to high school students who know that they have real chances to go to college, succeed and advance toward meaningful careers. We know because we listened to parents who told us (in English and Spanish) about the new hope they have for their sons and daughters because neither they nor anyone else in their families had graduated from high school, much less attended college. We know because we saw the college acceptance letters, the SAT and ACT scores, the debate trophies, the drama awards, the student research presentations and hundreds of other artifacts of student learning and success. We know ultimately, because the students at all four schools convinced us that their schools were designed to accomplish both the spirit and the letter of the Pace motto: Educate Students, Graduate Leaders, Empower Communities.

References

Bandura, A. (1977). Self-efficacy: Toward a unifying theory of behavioral change. *Psychological Review, 84,* 191–215.

Bryk, A., Sebring, P. B., Allensworth, E., Luppescu, S., & Easton, J. O. (2010). *Organizing schools for improvement: Lessons from Chicago.* Chicago, IL: University of Chicago Press.

Chenoweth, K. (2007). *It's being done. Academic success in unexpected schools.* Cambridge, MA: Harvard Education Press.

Chenoweth, K., & Theokas, C. (2011). *Getting it done: Leading academic success in unexpected schools.* Cambridge, MA: Harvard Education Press.

City, E., Elmore, R., Fiarman, S., & Teitel, L. (2009). *Instructional rounds in education: A network approach to improving teaching and learning.* Cambridge, MA: Harvard Education Press.

Edmonds, R. (1979). Effective schools for the urban poor. *Educational Leadership, 37,* 15–24.

Goddard, R. D., Hoy, W. K., & Hoy, W. A. (2000). Collective teacher efficacy: Its meaning, measure, and effect on student achievement. *American Education Research Journal, 37*(2), 479–507.

Goddard, R., Hoy, W., & Hoy, A. (2004). Collective efficacy beliefs: Theoretical developments, empirical evidence, and future directions. *Educational Researcher, 33*(3), 3–13.

Hattie, J. (2009). *Visible learning. A synthesis of over 800 meta-analyses related to learning.* New York: Routledge.

Hattie, J. (March, 2017). Collaborative Impact. Keynote Address given at the Collaborative Impact: Research & Practice Conference. Retrieved from: https://visible-learning.org/2017/05/video-john-hattie-collabora tive-impact/

Johnson, J. F., Perez, L. G., & Uline, C. L. (2012). *Teaching practices from America's best urban schools: A guide for school and classroom leaders.* New York: Routledge.

Johnson, J. F., Uline, C. L., & Perez, L. G. (2017). *Leadership in America's best urban schools*. New York: Routledge.

Leithwood, K., Louis, S. K., Anderson, S., & Wahlstrom, K. (2004). *How leadership influences student learning*. New York: The Wallace Foundation.

Marzano, R. J. (2001). *Classroom instruction that works*. Alexandria, VA: ASCD.

Marzano, R. J. (2003). *What works in schools: Translating research into action*. Alexandria, VA: ASCD.

Marzano, R. J., Waters, T., & McNulty, B. A. (2005). *School leadership that works: From research to results*. Alexandria, VA: ASCD.

Purkey, S. C., & Smith, M. S. (1983). Effective Schools: A Review. *Elementary School Journal*, 83, 426–52.

Rivkin, S. G., Hanushek, E. A., & Kain, J. F. (2005). Teachers, schools, and academic achievement. *Econometrica, 73*(2), 417–58.

Sanders, W. L., & Rivers, J. C. (1996). *Cumulative and residual effects of teachers on future student academic achievement*. Knoxville, YN: University of Tennessee Value-Added Research and Assessment Center.

Valenzuela, A. (1999). *Subtractive schooling: U.S.-Mexican youth and the politics of caring*. NY: Suny Press.